D0075666

PRIVACY

PRIVACY

A Manifesto

WOLFGANG SOFSKY

Translated by Steven Rendall

PRINCETON UNIVERSITY PRESS
Princeton & Oxford

Library of Congress Cataloging-in-Publication Data

Sofsky, Wolfgang.
[Verteidigung des Privaten. English]
Privacy : a manifesto / Wolfgang Sofsky ; translated by Steven Rendall.
p. cm.
Includes bibliographical references (p.   ).
ISBN: 978-0-691-13672-1 (cloth : alk. paper)
1. Privacy. I. Title.
BF637.P74S74513   2008
323.44'8—dc22   2008019960

British Library Cataloging-in-Publication Data is available

This book has been composed in Fairfield LH

Printed on acid-free paper. ∞

press.princeton.edu

Printed in the United States of America

10 9 8 7 6 5 4 3 2 1

Contents

PRIVACY

1 TRACES

By the time Anton B. left the building in the morning, he'd already been recorded three times. His conversation with his parents had been saved on a telephone company computer. He entered the field of a surveillance camera in the hall the moment he stepped out the door of his apartment. As he was hurrying to the elevator with his four-year-old son, on the ground floor the doorman was going toward the revolving door. Holding one hand behind his back and fumbling with the top button of his blue uniform coat with the other, he smiled at B. and gave him a nod. Before he made his next round he straightened his tie and quickly wrote in his record book the time at which B. had left the building.

As B. drove toward the kindergarten, he noticed that the needle on the gas gauge was getting close to the red area. It looked as though new devices had been hung over several intersections during the night. Only at the gas station did B. still see the old video cameras. Now and then the cashier looked over at a little screen that never showed anything but cars, gas pumps, bored passengers, and customers moving around. As usual, B. paid for his gas with his credit card. On the receipt were listed not only the gas but also the newspaper and a bag of licorice that B. handed to his boy, who was begging for the candy. When they got to the kindergarten a few blocks farther on, his son immediately ran happily into the big playroom where a clown's head was mounted on a swivel on the ceiling, its glass left eye peeping down at the room. If B. wanted to see what his son was doing he needed only to boot up the computer in his office.

B. turned on the car radio and put on his sunglasses. Because he was in a hurry, he floored the gas pedal and quickly turned onto the expressway. He had been driving this route for years and knew exactly where the radars were. So he was all the more surprised when he saw a flash as he drove up the on-ramp. Cursing, B. pounded on the steering wheel. Then he remembered that on the toll bridge all license numbers were filmed and compared with those of stolen cars. He didn't notice the infra-red flash on the pedestrian bridge. Even before he'd reached his company's underground garage, almost every instant of his existence in the public sphere had been recorded. He entered his office using a card with a computer chip that recorded his arrival time.

B. sat down at his desk and turned on his computer to look at his e-mails. Between the computer and the keyboard there was a little device that recorded all his keystrokes. Although B. was in a position of trust, a key-logger was installed on his machine as well. Employees were allowed to use the Internet, even for their own purposes, but they had to remember that everything they keyed in would be recorded. Most of them therefore vol-untarily avoided using the company's computers for their private correspondence. The inconspicuous device on the keyboard reminded everyone that, so far as possible, he should keep his secrets to himself.

During the lunch hour, B. got two calls. His tax adviser reported that tax officials had requested a statement regarding a foreign payment. B. was not aware of any irregularity. Apart from a few parking and speeding tickets, he'd never had any problem with the authorities. However, a year earlier he'd used his credit card to pay the bill at the hotel where he'd spent his vacation. The inquiry suggested that the tax man knew everything that happened in his bank account. Obviously some official had looked into his affairs without notifying him about it. B. felt a vague concern welling up inside him. He opened the window and looked down on the narrow street below. Music was being played softly over a loudspeaker. Now and then he could hear a strange buzz. It came from a tiny, almost invisible surveillance drone listening for suspicious noises in alleys and side streets.

The second telephone call was from his family doctor, who asked which data B. wanted to be recorded on the new health card. In order to make emergency care easier and decrease costs, the health insurance companies had recently begun to issue each patient a card with a computer chip, on which, along with identification information, all previous diagnoses, treatments, and prescriptions were registered along with an organ-donor agreement. The doctor advised B. to put only the required minimum of information on the card, a proposal that B. immediately accepted, even though he believed the trend toward complete digital records was ultimately unstoppable.

About 1:00 PM B. inquired about a train connection for his wife, who was visiting her parents. On the phone, his father-in-law promised him that he would not fail to get his daughter to the train station on time. B.'s company had expressly allowed private calls to be made on B.'s business phone. However, all area codes and numbers were recorded for the monthly telephone bill. In any case, the walls of the offices were so thin that they discouraged conversations that were too confidential or long-winded. B. had long since learned not to mention names when he was on the telephone. But it didn't take a genius to guess the names from the characteristic but inevitable expressions used in a conversation. Around 4:30 PM, he turned off his computer, put his things in his briefcase, stuck the card with the computer chip in the reader, and descended into the underground garage.

Video cameras in the corridor and in the elevator allowed the company's security guards to know who was currently in the building. On the expressway B. passed the toll bridge and the pedestrian bridge again before he parked his car in the supermarket lot. Right behind the entrance stood an inconspicuous device the size of a refrigerator, a backscatter X-ray machine that scanned every customer. The screen showed not only what one might be hiding under one's clothes or underwear; one's naked shape also was clearly recognizable. Although B. regularly bought food for the family on his way home and knew every corner of the store, on this particular day he walked helplessly up and down the aisles. At the cash register he hesitated to pull out his credit card. Credit cost him dear. Every time he bought something, his preferences, whether he tried a new product, and how much money he probably could spend were all recorded.

At the train station guards in dark-blue uniforms checked all suitcases, backpacks, and handbags, sometimes cursorily, sometimes meticulously. The video cameras on the platforms were state-of-the-art. They had microphones and identification filters that triggered an alarm when they detected unusual movements or certain faces. After the recent incidents, railroad officials had hastily installed new devices. According to the official announcement, even the most experienced observer would have been unable to monitor thousands of passengers at the same time. Automatic comparison of the pictures with a photo and video databank, however, took only a millisecond. Using eyebrows, the distance between the eyes, the tip of the nose, and countless other physical characteristics, a suspicious face could immediately be spotted from any point of view. Neither glasses nor beards nor wigs could prevent identification. B. had read about all that in the newspaper. Nonetheless he wondered about a couple of uniformed guards who were no longer wandering around the waiting room, as they had done earlier, but were now standing conspicuously along the wall. Out of the corner of his eye he saw that at the end of a platform four guards had surrounded a young man. They were pushing him against a guardrail and searching him. Passersby paid little attention; a few looked the other way, and others pretended that they didn't see anything. One shouldn't get involved, people said, everything is all right. Minor arrests are arranged by the authorities.

On the way home, B. and his wife picked up their son at the kindergarten. When the family entered the apartment building, the staff had begun a new shift. The new doorman gave them a friendly smile and wrote down their arrival time. He glanced briefly at the monitor screen, and then went back to his crossword puzzle. B. hesitated for a moment. He found it almost impossible to go into the elevator; all of a sudden, it was as if he'd heard a voice that told him to wait. Only when he had closed the door to their apartment did he feel that he was no longer being observed.

After dinner he booted up his laptop and got on the Internet. Immediately he found himself again the object of attention. His Internet Service Provider recorded his activities. The Web sites he visited recorded his data. He had given his e-mail address to a newsgroup, and the auction site where he usually tried to complete his collection of antique toys had registered every one of his transactions over the past month and made them available to everyone who might be interested in them. Every ten minutes a window came up on his screen warning him that his virus definitions were out of date and needed to be updated immediately. Unknown Trojan horses might be collecting information on his computer. B. ordered two books from a bookstore that already had his credit card information. He checked the prices for digital cameras at three sites. His electronic mailbox contained several advertisements sent by companies he'd never heard of.

Before he went to bed, Anton B. spent a moment thinking over the events of the day. A brief malaise came over

him as he began to realize that he had not been alone for
even a minute.

∾

Most of our contemporaries are not aware that they are
constantly being watched. Surveillance technology and
the business of daily spying go on largely unnoticed. People have long since gotten used to video cameras, discount
cards, and advertising messages. Some of it seems tedious,
some of it inevitable, and much of it is invisible and unrecognized. Video cameras promise to provide security,
registration services offer convenience. Although it occasionally annoys him, the transparent citizen appreciates
how much easier life is in the computer age. He unhesi-
tatingly foregoes being unobserved, anonymous, unavail-
able. He has no sense of having less personal freedom. He
does not even see that there is something to be defended.
He attaches too little importance to his private sphere to
want to protect it at the expense of other advantages. Privacy is not a political program that can win votes. Protection of secrecy is not something that would be widely
supported in societies with excruciatingly pervasive public
spheres. The need to be left alone is not widespread. It
is in profound contradiction with the spirit of the time,
which sees everything as political and values being known
over privacy. But the lack of protest and the feebleness of
the defense do not mean that the danger is slight.

People leave more traces behind them than they realize. No longer is one allowed to withdraw from society and live without being pestered. The trail is so broad

that resourceful investigators can quickly determine where someone has been and with whom he has spoken. The individual cannot secretly change masks and become someone else. He can neither disguise himself nor temporarily disappear. His body is regularly X-rayed, his journey through life recorded, and his life changes documented. And the longer the data are stored, the less likely they will be forgotten. Archived knowledge is constantly growing. If necessary, any past event can be reconstructed. Nothing is overlooked, ignored, thrown away. Thus people are condemned to rely completely on themselves. They have to think about every trace they leave behind them, calculate in advance every consequence of their actions. When every careless act, every error, every fleeting trifle is recorded, there can no longer be any spontaneous action. Everything one does is evaluated and judged. Nothing escapes surveillance. The past suffocates the present, and no one dares to tackle the future anyway, because no one can take responsibility for every one of his preferences, for every time he is negligent or unreliable. If data were not erased at regular intervals, people would be imprisoned in the dungeons of their own history.

However, this outlook seems to frighten hardly anyone. Contemporary Western societies, it is said, are ruled by the law of change, of transience. Fashions come and go, acquaintances change, thoughts evanesce before they have even been worked out. Everywhere we find ourselves unwilling witnesses to empty discussions. The range, decibel level, and pace of communication have exploded.

Despite filtering programs, given the chaos of noise and images, no telescreen could reliably protect all suspicious traces. The primary concern is not private secrets but the public staging of oneself. According to the law of the media society, anyone who is not seen does not exist. What people fear is not that they will be observed but rather that no one will pay attention to them. Our contemporaries seem constantly to be busy clinging to images. Why should one be concerned about the video camera in the mall if one is hurrying from one snapshot to another and strikes a pose before every new background?

In the tumult of signs, some of our contemporaries resort to bizarre means to elicit respect and to leave some trace on the social memory. They pull out all the stops; their appeals are shrill and hysterical, their opinions abstruse and idiotic, their appearance strange and overdone. People want to appear on national television at any price, in order to display the banality of their lives before everyone's eyes. Once the spotlight is turned off, they melt unnoticed back into the crowd.

The vulgar quest for short-lived prominence is accelerating the destruction of privacy. The economy of attention makes people blind to the political danger. The yearning for personal significance has long since obliterated all sense of privacy. We therefore have no reason to regard the situation as one without danger. Worse yet, why bother with X-ray machines when people willingly expose themselves? Listening devices seem superfluous when one-on-one conversations constitute only a tiny fraction of communications, and when dialogue carried on by telephone, telex, or Internet can be recorded at any time. Does everything have to be bugged and recorded if the mass of everyday conversation conceals only a void of meaninglessness? Not even video cameras will be necessary if everyone begins carrying an identity card that shows where he is at every moment.

2 POWER AND PRIVACY

Power is always out to expand its domain. It seeks to take control over the last remaining free niches. It maintains its existence by drying up the sources of obstinacy and turning people into friendly neighbors and obedient subjects.

As soon as subjects stop resisting, power crystallizes into domination. Social and political domination is constituted not by norms and institutions but instead by people's conformism. It is not the rule as such but rather regular obedience to it that produces institutions. Obedience can be based on diverse motives: a calculation of the costs of disobedience versus the advantages of relinquishing freedom, simple fear, an unquestioned model drawn from the past, the aura of authority, belief in procedural legality, utopian hope, religious conviction, or cultural tradition. For the most part, the motives for obeying are mixed to the point of being indiscernible. Just as it is expedient to honor those whom one must fear, it is no less expedient to justify habitual powerlessness by the power of habit.

Sporadic reluctance does not alter submissiveness. The subject's grumbling does not change the fact that he is a subject. So long as he allows himself to be told where to go, how to live, what he is supposed to do, think, and have, domination is not challenged. The subject regains independence only when he begins to fight for lost ground and puts a stop to the master's attacks. The defense of privacy is the first step toward rescuing freedom. Publicity may force the master to provide proof and serve to constitute an opposition group. It has to reveal power's secrets and offer a forum where issues concerning everyone can be aired. Privacy, on the contrary, is the individual's fortress. It is an area free of domination, the only one under the individual's control. The private comprises what is no one else's concern. It is neither public nor manifest. The private is not for other eyes, ears, or hands; it is not shared with others and is not accessible to them.

People's claim to their own sphere is seldom respected by power. Privacy limits power's claim to be omnipresent. Even laws do not prevent power from campaigns against personal territory. However, the most brutal attacks take place in times of totalitarian arbitrariness. It is true that dictatorships have never been able to take possession of every brain or to penetrate all the ramifications of society. But internal resistance was crushed and ultimately had no prospect of success. Totalitarian regimes were destroyed not by resistance and revolutions but rather by mismanagement or military defeats. Neither fascism nor state socialism was brought down by the rebellion of those they oppressed.

Control went far beyond briefly examining private data or bringing people's ideas into line. Surveillance was always coupled with violence and persecution. Police states and single-party regimes took swift deterrent action. They preferred denunciations, arrests in the middle of the night, torture, dungeons, executions, and massacres. Whole groups of people were not only spied upon and expropriated but also labeled, deported, wiped out. The destruction of privacy was only the first step down the path toward the annihilation of the human being as such. Surveillance of enemies of the state, people, or class was nearly complete. Hardly anyone who was pursued got away. The number of the "just" was increasingly small. The organs of repression seemed omnipresent even for the majority that was faithful to the regime. Millions of informers and accomplices were employed to keep an eye on the rest of the country. Although the walls were not of glass, the party, block wardens, stool pigeons, and secret police were extensively informed of deviant opinions and underground activities; indeed, they located any opposition before it had even made a move.

When terror rules, power can carry out its investigations openly and use surveillance as a means of intimidation. Thus informers hung around outside the homes of known dissidents. You couldn't miss them. Their presence was a kind of threat. But, in any case, spying on subjects was an open secret. Everyone knew that countless agents were making inquiries, but no one knew what they already knew and whom they had infiltrated into their milieu. Informers usually lived unrecognized in social circles. Every fellow worker, every friend, one's spouse or one's own child could be a stool pigeon. The rulers had placed informers throughout the society. They were not content to collect pictures and rumors. The secret police used pieces of cloth to absorb people's odors, a proven criminological technique. Thousands of pieces of yellow cloth were preserved in mason jars. The odor-spies disguised themselves as Red Cross volunteers and went to events organized by the opposition. If someone asked for first aid, that person automatically left an olfactory trace on a piece of cloth that later allowed bloodhounds to identify him.

∾

The age of Big Brother saviors, cheering crowds, and malicious informers is long over. In Western countries, the danger of totalitarianism seems to have been averted. Today, we are told, it is not the mass man that rules but rather the cult of individualism. Horizontal networks and flat hierarchies have replaced coercion and cults of personality. Instead of a uniform life, a multiplicity of milieus and lifestyles has evolved. Imagination is not extinguished, and people seldom get flustered when a stranger suddenly appears.

All the same, the history of repression has by no means come to an end. Every kind of domination, whether democratic or autocratic, threatens the individual's freedom. These days, however, the attack on privacy is carried out in accord with justice, morals, and law. Transformations of domination are always accompanied by changes in the technologies of power. Totalitarianism attacked the private sphere, because it sought to eradicate any independent thinking. It used terror and privileges to protect the power structure. It drew its legitimacy from economic progress, utopian hopes, edifying experiences of community, and the value of providing guidance, which is characteristic of any order, even the most repressive.

In democracies, another law is dominant. Like any system of domination a constitutional state founded on the rule of law has a secret political police that is supposed to protect it against subversion. Even democracies are capable of engaging in witch hunts and snooping campaigns. Yet the political class is also under constant surveillance. It has to worry about whether its legitimacy will stand up when dangers to law and order loom. Since it has promised electors security and peace, it has to take preventive measures. In despotic states, subjects fear the arbitrary power of the master and his accomplices. In democracies, a citizen longs for the authorities to take care of him. He seeks protection not from the state but rather by the state. In case of danger he immediately demands that tighter controls be imposed. The greater the society's fear, the more energetic the state's intervention and the smaller the chances for freedom. For members of the ruling elite, imposing restrictions on privacy is a condition of survival. For them, any negligence means political death. One slip and they would immediately be voted out of office. To avoid even the appearance of not doing anything, they take the precaution of having real or alleged opponents tracked down and eliminated.

In the era of Joe McCarthy and J. Edgar Hoover, the United States was in the grip of panic over communist infiltration. Apprehension regarding a vast communist conspiracy was completely out of proportion to the actual danger. Countless people fell under suspicion and were investigated or excluded from certain professions. In Germany, after a series of terror attacks, surveillance was so sharply increased in the fall of 1977 that people who were not involved at all were arrested on the street. After the 9/11 terror attacks, many governments established secret services and passed patriotic laws that exempted executive powers from public supervision. In the United States, Muslim immigrants were generally suspect. They were put under surveillance and not a few of them were taken into custody on flimsy grounds. Simultaneously the National Security Agency recorded, without legal authorization, data regarding thousands of overseas phone calls. Telephone companies provided the authorities with the phone numbers, the length of the calls, and the times the calls were made but not what was actually said. But one doesn't have to listen to conversations to know what a person is up to. If every call is registered, one also knows each person with whom someone has spoken. This registration not only lays open the personal private sphere but also provides insight into the society's network.

The growth of the modern state has already been accompanied by an erosion of privacy. Increasingly the private has to be wrested away from the inner imperialism of state power. In the name of care and precaution, areas of freedom are constantly being further restricted. Without information, without documents and data, bureaucratic domination cannot exist. The state has never limited itself to ensuring freedom. It has always been concerned to expand its power, even on the pretext of contributing to the moral improvement of society. At the beginning of the twenty-first century, the state is far from allowing its subjects to lead their lives according to their own lights. The "iron cage of serfdom" has finally been realized.

Accordingly, privacy is ideologically suspect. Having apolitical beliefs, not voting, being indifferent to power games, refusing to applaud—these count as betrayals of democracy. Anyone who declines to play along with the power game is considered a political idiot, a traitor to the community, a philistine. He or she is accused of either retreating into a cozy corner or fleeing into the sphere of late-bourgeois high culture.

The popular slogan according to which everything private is political simply helps power achieve total control. In reality, the political coincides with neither the state nor the social world. Among the few achievements of modern civilization is the demand that the state remain within its bounds and that politics be prevented from encroaching upon society. The limits of the private are the limits of the political. The defense of privacy is the individual's most effective objection to the fatal universality of power. It springs from the insight that even when power is exercised by democratic elitism it has to be tightly controlled. Even majority rule, along with its spokespersons, its informers, its representatives, and its executives, is a form of domination. All the rhetoric about the equality of citizen voters simply conceals the real inequality of power. Thus political freedom is not least of all freedom from politics.

∾

Law alone cannot be relied upon. Its most important instrument is prohibition. Law is in no sense a power-free sphere. It is a medium and means of power. Its prohibitions amount to commands. They must be promptly obeyed.

A regime always ultimately seeks to restrict freedom, no matter what reasons it gives for doing so. The total state wants to guide society and educate its citizens. New rules and regulations are constantly being imposed on everyday life. Security and public health, the protection of threat-ened minorities or majorities that feel injured are not al-ways involved. By no means should people be protected against one another or the individual preserved from addiction or temptation. The politics of prohibition has long since invaded areas in which the potential damage is either a private matter or at most a matter of opinion.

The politics of prohibition makes use of deliberate para-logisms: just because something is not forbidden does not mean that it is permitted. What is not required is also not permitted; and, ultimately, what is permitted is only what is required. The rule of norms knows only requirements and prohibitions. Freedoms and permissions immedi-ately arouse suspicion. In a closed legal world there is no dispensation, and certainly no area free of norms. Every loophole in the law seems to the legal executive power to be an evil that must be immediately eliminated. Does the Devil's hideous face not peep out of every rent in the legal fabric? Where there is no norm, is there not a threat of crime, moral dissipation, going berserk?

The growth of offenses against law and order seems so obvious to subjects that they hardly notice the loss of private freedom. Speed is strictly limited, parking spaces rationed, access to city centers barred. Regulations set hours for shopping and consuming, prohibit free work, risky wagers, and strokes of gambling luck. People are expressly warned against pleasures, excessive cravings are denounced, and drug use, by which subjects sometimes free themselves of their burdensome selves, is severely punished.

Norms are supposed to set the limits of normality. But the politics of prohibition is based on a magical idea: you cure something by using something similar. Since evil works by infection, even the smallest source of infection has to be eliminated. Prohibitions are supposed to be a deterrent, since they threaten potential evildoers with punishment. Everyone should be able to live without fear. The goal of prohibitions is to lessen fear in society. But prohibitions use the fear of punishment to fight the fear of danger. Everyone can live without fear only if everyone fears punishment if he disobeys. The more prohibitions there are, the more fear. And the higher the threshold of concern, the more prohibitions. Thus prohibitions create the grounds for their own intensification.

Anyone who wants to draw public attention to a private bad practice has to forbid it. What looks like a policy of containment actually first draws attention to what it tries to contain. There is no prohibition that cannot be violated. In fact, the prohibition provokes the violation, because it exists in order to be violated. People will continue to indulge in drinking and gambling, in eating too much fat and smoking cigarettes. Legislatures foolishly believe that they can use prohibitions to eliminate evil from the world. The opposite is the case. Prohibitions first create the situation that they seek to prevent.

Prohibitions require constant surveillance. The state as the protector of morality—that is a program for employing hosts of whistleblowers, informers, and prosecutors. There is no norm without punishment. However, the

deterrent effect is minimal. Laws do not produce morality. Most wrongdoers think they won't be caught. It is always other people who are guilty of one's own vices. And
if someone is caught, he blames his difficult situation not
on himself but on the spies. The more norms there are,
the more offenses and the more extensive the supervisory
bureaucracy. The result of the state's politics of prohibition is not better morals but rather the growth of the state
apparatus.

∾

Surveillance has always been one of the most effective
methods of control. Fear of the gaze of the Other keeps
people submissive. This fact underlies all the discoveries
made by modern technologies of observation. For a long
time, an unexpected spot check was enough to ensure
compliance. All it took was an example made here and
there, a sudden inspection, a severe punishment, and the
whole country was quiet as a graveyard. Anyone who has
to reckon with the possibility of being watched will voluntarily conform. It used to be that power did not seek to
gain complete information but only to create chronic fear
of a sudden attack. In ages of discipline, video cameras do
not even have to be on to make subjects feel that they are
continually visible and vulnerable to attack.

But today power is unwilling to rely on fear of discovery, obedience, and loyalty to laws and principles alone.
Its suspicion of its subjects is too deep for that. It wants
to know everything, all the time, everywhere. The battle
against evil is never over. The new state shapes society
not by providing order and trust but by saturating it with

fear and mistrust. Prevention creates a climate of constant alarm. It detects violations of prohibitions everywhere. The state itself creates the problem that it claims to be fighting. If everything is supervised, then danger must be looming everywhere. If everyone is watched, everyone might be an offender. Who knows all the masks evil wears? The less conspicuous someone is, the more suspicious he seems. Making oneself inconspicuous has after all always been the best camouflage. And the greatest danger always lies in wait where everyone sees it but no one suspects it.

The general suspicion admits of no exceptions. But the more we know, the more we realize that we still don't know everything. Every gap in our knowledge demands further investigations. Hence large signs, television spots, and wanted posters warn citizens to keep an eye on one another. Suspicious individuals are to be immediately reported. Every subject is an agent of national security. These measures not only destroy the freedoms that they are supposed to defend but also drive individuals apart and sever their social ties. In the end, no one feels safe with others.

The transparent subject is only the latest model of political power. But the current expansion of supervision is only one measure. Power is not at all confined to information power. The defense of privacy goes far beyond protecting private data. It is a task set for every civilization. The boundaries of the private must be made secure over and over again. The freedom of privacy cannot be guaranteed by the constitutional state based on the rule of law but only by every individual actually keeping his own secrets. The right to privacy, to the inviolability of one's own body and sphere of life, is nothing more than an idea so long as it is not covered by people's resistance. But although it is politically indispensable, protest against legal or unauthorized investigation of personal information is not enough. Protest already pays tribute to the decline of privacy. Protecting the private sphere involves protecting one's own way of life, property, and room for maneuver. Privacy gives everyone the right to remain incognito in public, and not to declare adherence to political creeds. Privacy means that everyone can seek his own happiness, and do it in his own way. Privacy worthy of the name includes freedom of belief and thought, freedom from unwanted disturbance and harassment, from being pressured by the community, the society, or the state.

3 RETROSPECTIVES

The wall is one of humanity's most important discoveries, like the wheel, the plow, or writing. It provides distance and protects against attacks. Behind a wall the individual can lay down the weapons with which he customarily defends himself against the demands of the public. A wall guarantees personal freedom.

But what domains does this wall now enclose? For our contemporaries the answer seems clear: inside the wall is the refuge of the family, friendship, and leisure time; outside it, the pressures of society, vocational obligations, the demands of the community and state dominate.

Whatever everyone can hear and see is public. The boundary of the private is first of all a boundary of the senses. The presence of others who can also see and hear what we see and hear requires us to draw a line of demarcation. Our household, home, and social gatherings are private, and so are our pleasures and inclinations, vices and deviancies, secret treasures and convictions, tastes and beliefs. Many bodily practices and things that befall our bodies are considered to belong to the private sphere: reproduction, love, sexuality, illness, and death. And ultimately ideas and feelings, sensual pleasures, passions of the heart, memories, wishes, and dreams—nothing seems more private than people's inner lives, hidden and surrounded by the shell of the body.

The marking off of a personal life-space is in no way self-evident. Privacy is both a historical and an anthropological fact. History did not begin after the great fire of London, which was then Europe's largest city, when the middle class retreated into their houses in order to avoid being bothered by the wildness of the streets. There has never been a society in which people have not sought to occupy their own terrain and to defend it against attacks. Never in the cultural history of *Homo sapiens*, not even in roving bands of looters, have nakedness, sexuality, urination, or defecation been seen as public activities. That privacy was in short supply and could be achieved only with difficulty does not mean that there was no need for it. Bodily functions were performed so far as possible away from the public eye. Huts and houses were protected by fences, large rooms divided up by imaginary walls, naked bodies covered by imaginary clothes. Delicate private zones were not to be noticed, and certainly not observed.

No doubt the extent of the private sphere and its borderlines have varied over the ages. When there are loopholes in social supervision and political power is weak, the private penetrates all social domains. On the other hand, if the public sector expands, the private may shrink to a small oasis. Despite historical changes, the distinction between what is one's own and what belongs to others, between the private and the general, is part of the universal structure of the social.

Let us consider three examples from Western history. In ancient Rome, a clear and distinct difference existed between the public and the private. Indeed, the modern words for these terms are derived from the Latin *privatus* and *publicus*. The private was the area not regulated by rules set by public offices or institutions. Goods belonging neither to the people in general nor to an officeholder were private. There was no state religion, property could be freely transferred, and both sexes could get a divorce. Everyone remained free to change his place of residence or vocation, and sexual misdemeanors were regarded with tacit indulgence. On the other hand, collective praise and blame were meted out for private behavior. Rome's notables and senators were subject to the supervision of public opinion. Every marriage, every will, was critically evaluated. The ruling class supervised the lives of its members in the interest of their honor and privileges. Not even the emperor was safe from the public's vigilant gaze. Augustus had a report read in the Senate on the licentiousness of his daughter and his grandchildren. In the presence of his Praetorian guards, Claudius harshly criticized the scandalous behavior of the empress Messalina.

In the early Renaissance, local authorities regarded the private realm of the family with great suspicion. They developed the first laws defending the municipal public sphere against usurpation by private interests. In time, the authorities succeeded in penetrating the territory of clans and families. City administrations enacted rules for the construction of private buildings and houses. They limited the height of family towers, and structures overhanging the street were subjected to punitive taxes.

Wealth had to be declared to the municipal authorities so that they could regulate responsibility for domestic financial resources, the distribution of inheritances, and the forms of dowry. Legal codes limited husbands' power, determined the age of majority, and set rules for marriage ceremonies. Even sexual misbehavior such as incest, bigamy, and homosexuality was publicly punished. The authorities gave special attention to private decisions that had public consequences. Burials and weddings were regulated in detail: the number of guests, the time of the banquet, the value of the trousseau, and the wedding gifts. The official fashion guide prescribed exactly which belts, furs, rings, shoes, and buttons could be worn, the length of the gown's hem, and the amount of embroidery allowed. Luxury and corruption of morals were a matter of deep concern for the city fathers.

Local administrations had a powerful ally in the authority of the Church, which measured families against the ideal model of the Holy Family. Opening the door of one's house to strangers could lead to many a temptation. Extravagant living, vanity, and lustful touching endangered morals. But the inner realm of the family was also considered a suspicious terrain. Thus Franciscan and Dominican monks began to establish confidential relationships with the social elite. As educators, spiritual advisers, and confessors, they spread strict doctrines regarding the use of the senses. When confronted by sin, one had to cast down one's eyes; the faithful Christian had to be careful of what he said and what he heard. Canonical periods were set for eating and fasting, and conjugal rights had to be exercised only in an appropriate place and in a natural position. The private became an area of clerical asceticism. The family was considered the sanctuary of morals and the fount of Christian society.

The French Revolution launched an attack on private life unprecedented in the Western world. In the name of the nation, private interests were repressed. Political assemblies were open to all, but every salon, every social circle, every private group was immediately denounced. Clothing became a sign of one's convictions: the shabbier, the more patriotic. The true republican man had to wear a short jacket, the "carmagnole," and wide trousers, and the true republican woman had to wear striped clothing in the national colors. Anyone who did not sport the red, white, and blue cockade was risking his head. During the Terror, experiments were even made with a single citizen's costume. Soldiers and civilians alike were to wear uniforms. Ideological kitsch made its entrance into private areas. Porcelain, tobacco cans, mirrors, and chamber pots were decorated with revolutionary themes, allegories of freedom, and equality. Every citizen had to use the familiar form of address ("tu") when speaking with fellow citizens, and everyone subject to the new nation had to speak the same language. Standard French suppressed dialects. The family was removed from the Church's supervision and redesignated as a secular institution. Marriage ceremonies henceforth had to take place before municipal authorities. But the state also determined the obstacles to marriage. The rights of parents were restricted, since children belonged first of all to the republic, the state. Thus the divorce law passed in 1792 was unusually liberal. A marriage could be dissolved not only because of brutality or adultery but also because of "incompatibility of characters." The Napoleonic civil code later strengthened the husband's rights, and in 1816 divorce was again largely prohibited. The limited period of greater freedom was bought at the price of a general politicization of the private. The revolutionary state redefined the way that time was reckoned and conferred the appropriate names on the children of the future.

The history of privacy has never run straight. It has known relapses and leaps forward; sometimes it has gone back to earlier stages or opened up previously unknown areas. Periods of relative freedom have followed periods of intervention, supervision, and repression. The private sphere has repeatedly been compressed by the pressure of the collective, the society, or the authorities until people remembered how to evade official expectations and protect secrets from organized indiscretion. Furthermore, the distribution of privacy was not simultaneous in the hierarchy of classes. Whereas poor families, which were often large, were crowded into one or two rooms, the upper classes usually had spacious houses or apartments in which individuals had at least a corner, a room, or a tower that they could call their own.

Only disciplinary institutions were exempt from the change in times. In closed, constraining societies the individual never had a chance to lead his life by himself, whether in a cloister or workhouse, a mental institution, a clinic, a penitentiary, or a barracks. Even if individual inmates might temporarily be allowed to have their own corner or special task, total and ascetic institutions trained subjects and reshaped their characters. Over the centuries the rule of disciplinary power remained the same: isolation; training of the body, its actions and gestures; the compression of time; the endless repetition of rituals, exercises, and ceremonies; visibility from all sides; the documentation of any deviation; and a hierarchy of ranks and regular inspections to determine progress. The society behind walls was a uniform society without privacy. Even if individuals had secret thoughts and desires, the institutional order was ultimately overpowering. Not only did it determine behavior, but it also shaped thoughts, tamed passions, directed desires and dreams. It penetrated people's brains. It broke the backbones of many. The state and society still resort to this proven model of repression in order to control outsiders, punish offenders, and raise obedient subjects. Every city has such institutions. So long as power and social order are not threatened, the social cages are reserved for exceptional cases. However, in a crisis, they are filled up and extended until finally the whole society has been transformed into a prison.

4 FREEDOM AND PRIVACY

A person is free who is not attacked. Privacy is the citadel of personal freedom. It provides defense against expropriation, importunity, and imposition, against power and coercion. It keeps unauthorized persons out. The fortress ensures independence and self-determination. Invaders cannot penetrate its bastions. Access to personal information is barred, as is entrance to intimate areas.

Like all freedoms, privacy is first of all negative. Its walls are bulwarks against external intruders and internal traitors. It is defended by keeping one's secrets; it sets limits on outside interference and plans a buffer zone of social distance. A private man values distance. Because people are always vulnerable, they can constantly become dangerous to one another. Privacy finds its ultimate basis in the physical constitution of *Homo sapiens*. One person attempts to push another out of the way, to subject him, to limit his movements, to guide his feelings, his thoughts, and gestures, to gain power over his body or over his understanding. Thus in every society the individual has to maintain his position against encroachment. The private sphere keeps others at a secure distance and provides a person with a place in the world.

Attackers are legion. The host of would-be intruders ranges from concerned parents, distrustful relatives, and curious neighbors to self-appointed moralists, testers of tolerance, ambitious shapers of opinion, and people who will tell you what to believe, and on to tax collectors, informers, and social services inspectors. They all infringe on the individual's right to freedom, the right to be left alone.

The ramparts of privacy are not an area of peaceful harmony. In a free society there is no delirious, joyful brotherhood. One individual's freedom ends where that of another begins. One of the paradoxes of negative freedom is that one must continually fight for it. One cannot keep others off one's back without acting against them. Legal guarantees count for little if others do not accept them, and the state, under the pretext of justice, continually enacts laws that restrict freedom. Thus secrets must be secured against curiosity, and private reserves must be made inaccessible to intruders. Inwardly, the wall has especially to be defended against individuals' rebellions. The war of the sexes, sibling rivalry, and generational conflict rage within the private sphere as well. Not infrequently they seek support from allies outside the walls. They open the gates, call for legal assistance or partisan arbitration. And private people themselves occasionally go outside in order to be in the limelight and advance their personal interests in the public sphere—at the expense of those they have left behind.

∽

Among the worst enemies of freedom is, in addition to power, social condensation. It is determined by the society's degree of integration. Where everyone knows everyone else, privacy can scarcely be maintained. The more closely woven the social network is, the more oppressive the proximity of others. Conversely, the more loopholes there are in the social network, the greater the individual's freedom. So long as people live in closed groups with strong ties, in a remote village, a royal court, or a prison, their relationships are close and manageable. However, established groups and outsiders pay for this closeness with a loss of freedom. A change in one's social group seems impossible. Being completely integrated means being bound by social fetters. Nothing is hidden from the attention of neighbors, the clan, or the community. Everything private is public. Every offense against customs and etiquette is immediately noted. Freedom grows only when distance and mobility increase. Fleeting encounters with strangers allow people to avoid giving detailed accounts of their inner lives. No one inquires into their personalities, their social status is irrelevant, and their rank is often not even discernible.

Anonymity is indispensable for protecting privacy. On the village street people meet who know each other. They greet each other and exchange a few words, even if only because politeness requires them to do so. Stories make the rounds, news is reported, gossip strengthens the bonds between locals and initiates. Walking down a street in a large city is an entirely different experience. Many people move through shop-lined streets without saying a word, making their way through the crowds, briefly sizing up the completely strange faces hurrying toward them, now and then stepping aside to avoid collisions. Subjects of conversation between strangers are limited. One can ask what time it is or how to get somewhere, and, when all else fails, discuss the weather. On such occasions, only people from rural areas explain whom they intend to visit and why they can't find them. They forego anonymity because in an inhospitable environment they are looking for signs of trust.

The historical site of the modern private sphere is the large city. There the opposition between public and private is sharp and clear. In the marketplace for goods and vanities, what counts is not the individuals but the buyers of things and the sellers of themselves. In the exchange of values, the customer goes from stand to stand, from shop to shop. No one has to know the other person, but everyone can enter into contact with him. Acts of exchange are fleeting and meetings are arbitrary, for when one has money in his pocket he is free. Countless private individuals move about in the marketplace. Everyone can come in. The private home is sharply marked off from the marketplace. It is reserved for its inhabitant alone. Even if it sits on a small lot and cost little, it provides a home. Inside a person's own walls no one can dictate what he must or must not do.

∾

Only when private matters are left to the individuals concerned can a multiplicity of lifestyles develop and make a society colorful and dynamic. Social diversity dwindles in proportion to the degree of outside intervention. The pressure of public opinion tends to homogenize attitudes and ideas. Prescriptions suppress free, independent activity. Outside instruction, outside direction, outside aid all deprive the individual of the incentive to find solutions by himself and use his own abilities to implement them. Every restriction on freedom attenuates the energy of action and keeps people from having a chance to feel the excitement of doing something by themselves. Whatever a person has not himself chosen and in which he is limited and guided is not incorporated into his self-confidence. It remains alien to him. Free, independent activity is also indispensable for social diversity and personal growth.

Like any freedom, privacy does not guarantee the moral good. In its hidden dungeons many strange inclinations thrive. People's likings are seldom valuable, virtuous, noble, or beautiful. Astonishment at the banal preferences of many private individuals is based on a confusion of freedom with morality. Freedom is not a virtue but rather the presupposition for any virtue. However, so long as no one is harmed or deprived of his freedom, private matters are out of bounds. What concerns a private person is no one else's business. Privacy—like freedom—is a value people cherish for its own sake. It is not a means to an end but rather an end in itself.

Every individual has a hereditary right not to make use of his freedom. No one is obliged to actually exercise the freedom offered by the private sphere. No one is required self-critically to secure his wishes and actions. No one is condemned to exploit his talents, improve himself, or even become a better person. It is completely impermissible to limit the private sphere simply because people refuse to strive for allegedly higher values. Someone who doesn't make something of himself is just as worthy of private freedom as one who purposefully seizes the opportunity to realize himself. An individual's abilities are not public property. Someone who does not make full use of his potential is not thereby squandering a public good.

People themselves know, better than any authority, what is good for them. Paternalism is an evil product of state pessimism. It is based on the erroneous belief that people are incapable of taking care of themselves and recognizing what is good for them. The modern state, on the pretext that it is only doing what is best for people, intervenes in everything, even against the express desires of the ruled. Taking precautions and providing care are no more than flimsy pledges. The state is neither bulwark of mores nor a moral institution. It does not protect a common good and is not a source of fatherly security. The state is an institution for dominating citizens. Their freedom diminishes as the extent of recording and the number of government employees grows. Far from making progress toward morality, the state's development moves in only one direction—toward an increasing disenfranchisement and expropriation of its citizens. The justice it claims to achieve requires more and more laws, the laws require more and more employees, and these employees require more and more money from the citizens, who always mistakenly hope that they will provide greater justice. The fortress of privacy, therefore, does not protect citizens alone. It also shields state power from the temptation to constantly expand instead of concentrating on the sole task for which it is fit: ensuring freedom.

5 TERRITORIES OF THE SELF

A person's integrity does not begin with the recognition of his independence or his conscience. Its core is not found in a person's dignity or honor but rather in his being left alone. Before the inviolability of the person stands the inviolability, the untouchability, of his skin. Therein lies the nerve center of everything private.

People fear nothing more than being grabbed from behind. Suddenly one feels a heavy hand on one's shoulder; one jumps, ducks one's head, crouches to reduce the vulnerable surface. It is like a predator's attack. The body is instantly in another condition. A lightning bolt runs through one's limbs, one's brain quakes, hot impulses race along the nerves. One seems helpless against the assault. Sometimes people still try to wriggle away, but usually slightly increased pressure on the neck is enough to keep them down for good. They are taken away without resisting further. They go quietly, as if a single act had suddenly deprived them of all strength.

The capture takes place without the brutal use of force. No blood is shed, no joint dislocated, no muscle, no artery, no nerve crushed. No one is injured. It is not for nothing that people have a primeval fear of being touched by others. The experience of being grabbed contains the most ancient dread. Surprise immediately flips over into panic. Fear and impotence are one.

This dread has its root in the nature of the human tactile sense. We experience our skin in a special way. The skin is what is deepest within us and at the same time our surface. When it is touched the organism reacts far more strongly than to any verbal or optical stimulus. No other sense can arouse us so much as the sense of touch. No other organ triggers such strong and contradictory feelings as the skin. Desire, shivering, pain, confusion are all immediately connected with the physiology of the skin. The skin wraps itself around life; it is our largest organ. It protects us against cold and heat; it is elastic, washable, and waterproof, but at the same time extremely sensitive and vulnerable. It encloses a person, gives him his unique form, and shields him against intruders. The sense of touch is the first human sense to become active, and it is the last to go. It remains awake at night, ready to receive impressions. The skin does not sleep. Like a sentinel, it protects the sleeper. Even in deep slumber it immediately reacts to touch. It causes the body to move away or to startle awake.

Touching other bodies produces feelings of security and closeness but also repulsion and reluctance. Through our skin we experience the separation between outer and inner. The skin is a living borderline, marking the difference between the ego and the world. It communicates directly the experience of one's own actions and suffering. The skin lies midway in the spectrum of the senses, between the conditions of taste and smell and the objects of seeing and hearing. But whereas an intervening distance exists between events and what our eyes and ears register, touch affects the subject directly. It leaves no possibility of flight. Alien fingers probe what will soon belong to the intruder. Is not the groping clutch followed by something stuffed in the mouth, chewed up, devoured?

The skin is sensitive in two ways. Through it we achieve the ability not only to live and experience but also to experience our experience. We acquire a relationship to ourselves by touching ourselves. Doing so provides us with an internal image of our external shape and a sense of the unity of our bodies. If the right hand feels the left, the left in the same way feels the touch of the right. And so the greater the irritation if the left hand has suddenly gone numb and no longer feels the touch of the right. The right hand, however, still feels the left but as a lifeless, material thing, no longer part of the same body. Thus it often takes people a long time to adjust to prostheses, until the foreign element is integrated into the body. Conversely, if the skin is touched by someone else's hand, without the ability to touch it in turn, the interplay of the sense of touch is also impossible. The body all at once feels a foreign power. It can snuggle up to it, resist it, or try to escape it. Unwanted touching is clearly an act of domination. It seizes the person totally.

It is not for nothing that in all cultures touching is subject to strict conventions. Only lovers, and mothers and their children, are allowed to touch each other without restrictions. Otherwise detailed rules govern which parts of the body may be touched and which may not. When people touch, it is as if they are addressing each other by their first names. Some infringements amount to regular pollution. In cramped situations we are allowed to touch one another with elbows or shoulders, but bodily fluids and orifices are generally off limits. A free civilization guarantees people that they will not be grasped or soiled. It ensures that distance is maintained and desires are restrained.

∾

The shell of the skin represents the outline of the body. It holds the individual in an indivisible possession. The human shape is surrounded by its personal space, an invisible sphere whose scope changes with population density and the social and material situation. In seconds, this mutable personal reserve can expand or contract. In an empty space, in a railway compartment, at a table in a restaurant, or in an elevator, an individual at first has a place for himself alone. But if a second person enters the elevator, the two have to share the space and adopt an easily defensible position—their backs up against the wall, usually on opposite sides of the car. Additional people entering the elevator position themselves so everyone has enough room, but each new passenger causes the others to reposition themselves, until finally they are all packed closely together, their arms pressed to their sides, their heads turned this way or that so as not to bother the others with their breath or their gaze. Constrained in this way, each individual treats the others as present non-persons. Involuntary eye contact is immediately excused by a friendly smile that signals an absolute lack of hostility. As the elevator empties out from one floor to the next, the cycle is repeated in reverse. Passengers move away from each other, the distance between them increases, and each seeks a secure place against the wall. The last one in the elevator moves once again to the middle, as if wanting once more to occupy the car for himself alone. Personal space takes advantage of opportunities, its boundaries are mobile, and yet members of a culture have a precise sense for over-familiarity, for the violation of the individual in the public sphere.

An individual's personal space accompanies him through the social world. This mobile stratum of his private sphere is connected directly to his body. Things are different, however, in the case of the delimited spaces or "boxes" in everyday life that one can temporarily leave without giving up one's claim on them. Seats in theaters, bars, or classrooms; lounge chairs on the beach or on boat decks; standing room at concerts or stadiums; carrels in libraries; park benches along a lake; corner seats in the canteen or in one's own garden; workplaces at machines, in the office, in vehicles, or in the kitchen—all these fixed boxes are marked by a claim on space. So long as the person using them is nearby, no one else is allowed to move into them. Small signs indicate that the box is occupied. People put down their bags, spread out their belongings, or occupy part of the seat beside them, thus warning others who want to occupy this box that they can expect impolite gestures, perhaps even contamination. Restricted boxes are relatively stable microspaces for the individual. As usually occupied, they are kept open and in case of need immediately surrendered. Some boxes are used as workplaces, others only as places to be. In the mobile world, they offer the individual a reliable, fixed point amid a fluctuating public sphere.

Proprietary reserves include personal possessions directly connected with someone: jackets, caps, gloves, packs of cigarettes, lighters, umbrellas, newspapers, and handbags, including their contents. The loss of these items often produces enduring confusion; the search for them frequently is an exasperating waste of time. It is a matter not only of these items' use value but also their value in relation to one's identity. Only unwillingly do we let go of the self's sacred objects. They are neither lent nor sold. Although often they are worth little, they accompany us through the perils of everyday life. They constitute the material infrastructure of our identities. They provide continuity when situations change. They endure beyond fleeting encounters and make us feel that we are surrounded by familiar things.

∾

A person's territory can be violated in many ways, through invasions and interventions, through arrogance, importunity, impoliteness, through soiling or sheer violence. First of all, foreign bodies are placed so close to us that they restrict our personal space. Alien hands are not kept within bounds—the well-intentioned clap on the shoulder, the unwanted hug, covert touching and groping. Then there are the penetrating stares fixed on others, feeling them out, eating them up. And the lascivious glance that at first surreptitiously and then impudently disrobes its victim. Calibrating one's gaze is a delicate task. The difference

between being attentive and being importunate is sometimes only a matter of seconds.

And then there are the interventions through words
and sounds, the disturbing noises, grunting, lip-smacking,
tongue-clicking, the futile gossip, grumbling, and coarse
laughter. In a civilized society, one needs permission to
address a stranger, even if only with an inconspicuous
nod. Some people's voices are so penetrating that they are
impossible to shut out. They turn others into unwilling
listeners. In contemporary society, loud people usually
don't notice how much they bother those around them
with their ringing cell phones, bellowing conversations,
boom boxes, roaring exhaust pipes, thunderous music, or
slamming doors. This acoustic environmental pollution is
often the result of sheer thoughtlessness. But the noisy
intruder is seen less as a troublemaker than the person
who does the complaining.

Finally, among the most unpleasant kinds of pollution
are the odors and excretions of others: spittle, mucus,
sweat, defecation, blood, sperm, flatulence, bad breath,
cheap perfume, scraps of food, stains on the tablecloth.
Such sticky or fluid traces commonly make us feel disgust
and aversion. Our stomachs turn; the body defends itself
against attack by trying to expel something. It preserves
the borderline between the ego and the world though an
involuntary impulse of rejection. The disgusting is not
something that confronts us, something we can hear or
see. It is of the most importunate intimacy. It sticks to the
skin, nestles up to us, blurs the dividing line of the body;
it penetrates us. The stench takes possession of the nose
and spreads inside us. We can defend ourselves against it

only by resolute acts. By ostentatiously holding our noses, we inform others that we cannot smell them.

Respect for the preserve of the senses is an achievement of civilization that is constantly in danger. Although cultures have different criteria of pollution, every society regulates the movements of the body by means of conventions, markings, and taboos. Arab men customarily look intently into each other's eyes while talking, stand very close, even touch each other. Someone who is repelled by an acquaintance's breath shames himself. On the other hand, a Japanese individual finds a Western European pushy as soon as the latter moves closer during a conversation. But the European finds the Asian cold or unfriendly as, inch by inch, the Asian backs away. Whereas in Central Europe an arm's length is considered a comfortable distance, in Russia and some Balkan countries people commonly grasp each other's arms when greeting. The hands are thereby put out of commission. Brotherly kisses on the cheeks or mouth emphasize peaceful intentions. Among white Anglo-Saxons, however, such intimacies arouse suspicion of a sexual relationship.

Conventions change over time. Eras of politeness give way to periods of vulgarity in which good manners are denigrated as deceptive parodies, hollow shells, or ludicrous window dressing. When spontaneity determines social contacts, protective rituals are no longer in force. In the name of truthfulness, the new community, or revolutionary brotherhood, people are allowed to pester each other directly. They call each other by their first names, eat in natural ways, besiege each other with amorous outbursts, and report every outlandish idea. Since property counts for nothing, requests or thanks are also not needed. Among the new brothers, disgust is seen as a relic of snobbism. Distinction and refined taste are considered reactionary. When everyone loves everyone else, any reserve is scorned. Everything belongs to everyone, and everyone belongs to everyone—that is the motto of a community in which everyone's self terrorizes others.

Politeness and etiquette keep people at a distance, not by virtue and morals but by the demands of form. The rule always precedes the moral, because virtue commonly arises first out of a painful repetition of the concept that gives people the habit of observing form. Manners precede morality; respect and imitation come before duty. Any contempt for manners fails to recognize the value of politeness for the growth of the moral person. It is useless to preach morality and instruct people in their duty so long as they have no practice in keeping their distance from others in accord with duty. It is true that good manners do not necessarily lead to generosity and gratitude, to uprightness and kindness. But at least they produce the appearance of these virtues. They make people appear outwardly what they should be inwardly. And they allow them to put up with one another even if they despise each other. Politeness conceals the natural vices of the species. It helps us to get over the dismal insight into the modesty of human beings' basic equipment by keeping us from seeing that most of our contemporaries are mediocre in stature. Etiquette preserves the fictions of philanthropy and, conversely, allows us to be in contact with our fellow humans without loving them. Manners ensure a peaceful coexistence, where dislike and hostility remain within bounds. Politeness suppresses overt attack through good manners. By refining crude involuntary gestures into deliberate courtly ones, conflict and violence are averted. The self-imposed pressure of good behavior conceals passion, and yet the illusion is often a salutary one because it creates the necessary distance. Politeness evens out coldness, coarseness, and indifference. And it protects us against false intimacy and false community.

In more restrained eras, bodies moved away from each other. Decorum demanded that feelings be tamed, emotions controlled, and the vicissitudes of the soul concealed from others. Instead of uninhibited openness, what counted was self-control, shame, and secrecy. It was permissible at one time to spit on the floor in the presence of others; covering the sputum with one's foot was sufficient. Today it is a gross offense to spit while engaged in conversation. In informal times, one could yawn as long as one wanted, assuming one did not talk while doing so. Today, in better circles, it is considered highly impolite to yawn during a conversation, as one thereby shows that one finds one's interlocutor boring. For a refined nose, the smell of other people's sweat elicits disgust, whereas in the past people were not so concerned with cleanliness, even in society's upper strata. Toilet water was more popular than water, that dangerous stuff that could seep in everywhere.

When one reduces bodily contact, shame and embarrassment loom. Unintentional infringement on the required distance is atoned for by excuses, explanations, or polite requests. Social accidents and territorial collisions often trigger a rite of reconciliation that restores order to the bodies concerned and strengthens the claims to private space.

These corrections usually take place without friction. But if the upset cannot be immediately calmed, people may resort to parting shots. As the offender leaves the scene of his crime, the injured party disparages him, sotto voce, so that only those nearby can hear. Behind adults' backs, children will stick out their tongues or give them the finger. Drivers with their windows rolled up can express their feelings freely for the benefit of their passengers while the object of their scorn is long since out of reach. These gestures preserve self-respect, which is directly endangered by every encroachment. The de-civilizing of manners always entails a destruction of the private. The end of politeness also means the destruction of freedom and social security.

∽

The threat to the realm of intimacy increases dramatically whenever encroachments are backed by legitimate power. The classical destruction of the personal preserve has always been arrest. The authorities take power over the subject's body. The hand on the shoulder, the police armlock, handcuffs, the body bent at the hips—the forces of order often act more roughly than necessary. Some delinquents allow themselves to be led away without resisting, but arrest does not mean merely that one is taken into custody. It is intended to inform the prisoner that he is entirely in the hands of the government. Being abruptly awakened, the rough paw shaking the shoulder, the dazzling flashlight in the eyes all deprive the victim of any opportunity to defend himself. Being arrested at dawn or in the half-light of a side street communicates a disturbing message. Attentive residents immediately know what's going on. In no case must the prisoner pass between the lines of curious onlookers with his head held high. He must immediately disappear from society. He is held by the arms on both sides and hurried to the police car. Even if there is no risk that he will attempt to escape or resist arrest, his body is put in restraints. Power is not content with symbols alone. Freedom of movement is denied, the taboo on touching is lifted. It is permissible to do things to the body of a person under arrest that would immediately arouse loud protests in civil life. The authorities have nothing to fear. They are in the great majority. Inconspicuous punches in the ribs, growls and curses, all tear the suspect out of his familiar world. Tight handcuffs cut off the blood flow. Sometimes the prisoner is forced to undress. Helpless and naked, he is placed in the hands of power. With the individual's personal space destroyed, power becomes tangible to him and catapults him into complete helplessness.

Often arrest is accompanied by a body search. Not only are closets, cars, and trunks rummaged through. The suspect must stand against a wall and spread his arms and legs wide so he can be frisked without danger. Or he has to empty his pockets and spread out all his intimate possessions. This practice, meanwhile, though originating in the police station, has been extended to the whole society. Perfectly respectable people are searched in countless places. At national borders, the thresholds of public rooms, in movie theaters, train stations, restaurants, and airports, security agents rummage through handbags, backpacks, pants pockets. Detectors are passed along clothing and, upon finding a metal object—a key, pocket knife, or wristwatch, immediately set off an alarm. Back-scatter X-ray machines not only show the naked human figure but also display, in addition to fluids and objects, the person's proportions. Some travelers are even subject to a physical body search. They are examined all over with nimble hands. Before they can protest, the procedure is over. But the unpleasant feeling of having been put into strange hands for a moment remains. Private possessions are fingered and evaluated with gloves that already have handled dozens, even hundreds, of private possessions. The agents see things that do not concern them. Polite supervisors keep the situation under control by offering excuses or explaining that the procedure is unavoidable. Others make do with a shrug or a friendly joke. But a third group of monitors keeps its distance from this unpopu-lar work and spontaneously allies itself with those being checked. The more patiently the latter allow themselves to be scrutinized, the easier it is to carry out the proce-dure. If agents are suspicious, however, the measures are sharply intensified. The delinquent must undress and un-dergo a body search. Drug couriers are known to transport their freight inside their stomachs or intestines. When all the luggage has been searched, inside the body seems to be the safest and final hiding place.

6 SECRETS OF THE BODY

Before people allow themselves to be seen by others, they correct their appearance. They prepare their entrance on stage even if only for spectators in their own family. The most important medium of social theatrical art is the body, its secrets carefully guarded and equipped with all sorts of props. Self-presentation is prepared backstage, and after the performance the mask is taken off again. The theater's dressing room is like the bathroom in a private residence, a place of secrecy and intimacy. Here individuals can inspect themselves unobserved, check out the distortions of their figures, touch up skin blemishes, whiten teeth, make their faces more attractive. Some contemporaries spend hours in this place of narcissistic worship. They experience critical moments when all the beauty aids are removed, and they see themselves without wigs, prostheses, or rouge. The bathroom is a place of unadorned self-encounter. There is a reason why many people insist on locking the bathroom door. Along with the bed, the bathroom is the last refuge where one can let the outer shell fall and wipe away burdensome feelings of shame.

Shame does not originate in the social fear of humiliation, disrespect, or exclusion. It begins with a person's relationship to himself, to his own body. Shame rises up, overcomes, and penetrates the individual. He would like to turn away, hide himself, sink into the earth, make himself invisible—to others and to himself. The boundaries of the private spare the individual many an occasion for social shame. They put the "private parts" outside the general view. But sealing off the intimate in no way protects the individual from painful self-inspection. Only because he can feel ashamed of himself in his own eyes can he also feel ashamed of himself in the eyes of others. He can see himself as others see him only because he has first observed himself. The self precedes the social. Masking the face, concealing the genitals, disguising the body, trying to attain the ideal weight—all this is done not only to avoid being ashamed of how one appears to others. Even someone with no intention of ever being onstage does not want to blush when seeing himself in the mirror. There is a reason why shame is considered the quintessential private feeling.

Shame calls for concealment. For a time, whatever doesn't strike the eye can still be driven out of consciousness. But ultimately people can have only open secrets for themselves. Even someone who is utterly familiar with the art of representation and is able to fool himself can hardly fail ultimately to see what is hidden behind the facade. Thus a twofold secrecy with regard to others is healthier for one's inner equilibrium. It seeks to hide not only a blemish but also the very fact that something is being hidden, and this is a task requiring considerable attentiveness. Not even the slightest mistake is allowed. The makeup must be so perfect that nothing indicates the minor corrections. Clothing must fit so that undesirable bulges completely disappear. Wigs must be naturally dyed so that not a single hair betrays that they are wigs.

The same is true for other personal flaws. Inclinations toward cocaine, alcohol, or amphetamines, sexual perversions, long periods in psychiatric treatment or in prison— whatever is regarded as a shortcoming in a given social circle has to be hidden by means of skillful information politics. However, unlike the biographical past, current secrets are constantly threatened with exposure. The body is visible, cravings demand satisfaction, and, for the most part, simply keeping quiet does not provide sufficient cover. Being unmasked entails fateful consequences. Someone who must finally admit that he has something to hide immediately arouses curiosity. If his secret is ultimately discovered, he cannot avoid blushing with shame. Sometimes the embarrassing fact will be graciously ignored. But shortly afterward the whispering, gossiping, and character assassination begin. Then everyone else wants to know everything; they want to raise the curtain all the way. That is how the failed art of concealment ends up producing the catastrophe of social revelation.

∾

Physical secrets are legion. There are the tacit inclinations, the perverse lusts, masturbation, homosexual temptations, hidden affairs, and, not least, the free-ranging fantasies of obscenity and violence at the most intimate moments, when one is not entirely present. Not only is the unsaid among the secrets of sexuality but so, too, is palpable deception: feigned orgasms, pretense of intimacy, the false kiss.

Sometimes couples conceal secrets from third parties: the vain quest for a climax, premature ejaculation, a chronic lack of desire and emotion, sadomasochistic practices, and forbidden incest. The secret of an abortion or of recourse to medical means in order to conceive a child can keep couples together. Conversely, relationships with third parties sometimes lead to rifts. A homosexual husband leads a double life within and outside the family; a disappointed wife changes lovers and yet, to preserve appearances, clings to the safe refuge of her family. Earlier, partners shared their secrets with a confessor; today, they seek the help of a physician, psychologist, or counselor. Despite the media culture of indiscretion, people continue to make their way along the narrow crest separating truth from deception, lies from confession. They retain as much ignorance and cultivate as many errors as necessary for their social existence.

With growing longevity and declining fidelity, it is becoming clear that monogamy was a historical invention for people who did not live very long. But the rhetoric of ingenuous spontaneity does not protect us against deep injuries. Unconditional openness at one time was propagated when an affair or an infidelity had occurred. But acknowledgment does not change a betrayal, a breach of trust, or humiliation into something else. Worse yet, requiring truthfulness demands a higher degree of self-denial from the person betrayed. He or she must not only be understanding but must also honor the unfaithful partner's confession as a proof of trust. Ultimately the discovery of the secret only accelerates the insight that love doesn't last and one's partner is replaceable.

Families can degenerate into dark, devious places. The mantle of the private also shrouds misdeeds. Violence, ill-treatment, and lethal neglect of duty are hushed up, and the mental and physical abuse of children is denied until an outsider breaks the conspiracy of silence and reports what is happening. Despite strict laws and public speeches, the number of unreported cases of abuse is high. Private family solidarity protects the tormentor and leaves the victim alone.

The right to privacy finds its limit where there is a threat to the individual's freedom from injury, degradation, and coercion. The physician's or social worker's duty to respect confidentiality stops at crime. Secret accessories to a crime cannot claim to be exempt from punishment because of their private misery. Someone who fails to report a dishonoring, rape, or neglect does not deserve a lesser punishment merely because he has duties as a relative, lives in difficult circumstances, or is said to be socially immature. He has decided to be indifferent to his failure and bears full responsibility for it.

The use of illegal drugs is also surrounded by secrets. Many alcoholics hide bottles and do everything they can to conceal their addiction from their children, partners, relatives, and neighbors. When they have to explain another episode of drunkenness, they can always talk their way out of it or find an excuse. On the other hand, the people around the drinker have to lock up anything that might tempt him. Although alcoholism is often an open secret, it forces both parties to take discreet steps.

After centuries of free access, tobacco is now tolerated only as a private passion in many Western countries.

Alcohol is still accepted but only in small doses. Official public health policy tends to be increasingly prohibitive. Regular consumption of alcohol is considered an addiction, as is the use of many narcotic drugs. Young people who swallow pills, sniff cocaine, or shoot heroin usually do it secretly, and when their parents catch them, they say nothing or resort to confidential discussions with a physician. Even though social occasions may encourage people to enter the drug scene, for the addict his private relationship to his own body has priority. He does not share his excitement and pleasure with others but instead experiences them by himself. When he gets high, he is overcome by a rare, solitary happiness. Being high is first of all an individual state beyond society. The companionship of a drinking bout is not a collective delirium, and, in any case, hangovers are individual. Meanwhile, the addict is alone with his drug. When the effect wears off, he reaches for the drug again, at first to renew and increase his pleasure, and ultimately only to avoid the torment of withdrawal. Escaping addiction requires not only a fundamental detoxification and a change in one's social surroundings but also a radical revision of one's relationship to oneself. If the addict remains the same person that he was and returns to the milieu where he formerly used drugs, a prompt relapse is foreseeable.

∾

The gloomier sides of private existence are no longer taboo. There is much talk about death and illness. The therapeutic society has expanded, and there is now a counselor or an electronic fellow sufferer for every defect.

There are even treatises circulating that tell the dying how to exit gracefully. Death seems to have been de-privatized. Although many people hope to die at home, most now die in hospices or hospitals. And although it may be clear that the end is near, old habits of not speaking of death remain in force. A dying person must still pretend that he is not going to die. Those around him join in this pretense to protect him. Hospital staff act as though it were the patient's duty to remain alive, and medical procedures often serve chiefly to mask the patient's decline. Visitors hesitate to speak the truth and, as they leave, express the hope that the patient will soon recover, though they know perfectly well that it is a hopeless case. Thus the dying person remains alone with his fear and rebellion. He is deprived of saying good-bye, and society is deprived of its mourning.

Physical pain that does not lead directly to death already drives the individual out of the public sphere. People become imprisoned in themselves, in the cage of their own bodies. Pain is the first *principium individuationis*. Pain can be expressed but not represented or shared. It stubbornly refuses to be communicated. The contorted grimace, the curled-up body, the animal groaning do not represent pain but are themselves the pain. To hide his pain and spare others the feelings of shame and helplessness, the sufferer grits his teeth. He knows from experience that he cannot share his torment with anyone. No one can empathize with his condition; at most, others can only imagine what it feels like. There is a world of difference between experiencing pain and understanding it. Thus, hiding pain has a double meaning: while it spares others the vain effort to empathize, it also spares

the patient the miserable experience of his own desola-
tion. At the very moment that he urgently needs the help
of others, he is locked up in the prison of his own body.

Suicide and assisted suicide also belong to the domain
of the private. In the hidden areas of medicine, contrary
to official declarations, assisted suicide is more commonly
practiced than is generally acknowledged or thought.
Drugs that can delay the end are no longer administered,
life-maintenance systems are put on hold, no additional
attempts at resuscitation are made, or painkillers are increased to shorten the final stage. Relatives and friends
are told a story they can accept about the last moments,
and are relieved that they did not have to watch their
loved one die. A few terminal patients who still have their
faculties may reject further therapeutic measures; sometimes the physician even complies with the patient's wish
because he wants to avoid unnecessary costs or to do the
patient one final favor. Hospital staff, friends and relatives, the physician, and the dying person often occupy
a twilight zone where no one speaks openly and secretly
hopes that the others will understand. Legal formalization
through laws, statements, certifications, or the testimony
of witnesses is hardly sufficient to illuminate this twilight
area of the private. Ultimately death and dying are not a
matter for law or the state but rather for the individual.

No human act is more enigmatic than suicide. Only
the person who voluntarily ends his life knows why he is
doing so. His death leaves behind a void that survivors
immediately try to fill with feelings, fantasies, and explanations. Was it rejection, sacrifice, or an appeal? An act of
escape or of resignation? Looking back, people search for

signs of what was coming, motives and events that might have triggered the act. Some people who commit suicide, it turns out, have long thought about ending their lives and made secret preparations. Others, however, must have been suddenly overcome by the whirling vortex that drags people over the edge. A person gets up in the morning as usual, eats breakfast with his family, puts his papers in his briefcase, closes the door behind him, and realizes, abruptly, that he's had enough.

Suicide is the most private act of all, an antisocial act par excellence. Nothing can challenge the public more than an act that realizes individual freedom by definitively tearing a person away from society. Ending one's life is the most radical way imaginable of breaking with society. It is scandalous for society, which therefore immediately brings in its experts to find some psychological deficiency, some social problem or genetic flaw, on which to blame the irrevocable act. A desire to die, we are commonly told, arises from depression, social isolation, or political or economic crises. Social existence is no longer supported by habits. Society has degenerated into a desolate waste dominated by chance, without the protection of the community, without the restraints of enduring duties. A condition of social lawlessness ultimately leads to personal catastrophe. The price of freedom, it is claimed, is a feeling of isolation.

Does all this explain the scandal of the free choice to end one's life? The reference to mental or social fate is supposed to keep fears within bounds. By reinterpreting the arbitrariness of the final act as a challenge to society, this view deprives it of its obstinacy but tells us little about the motives leading a person to commit suicide.

Why one person chooses to escape into nothingness, and another, despite suffering the same emotional state, does not; why one person does not act but another lays hands on himself; what happens in the final hours, in the bathroom at home, in the unfamiliar hotel bed, in the car on the highway or on the bridge—no one can answer these questions. Few people, it seems, arrive at the decision to commit suicide by weighing the advantages of continuing to live against those of not doing so. In any event, who has the right to set criteria that can determine for other people when it is permissible for them to voluntarily end their lives?

∽

Secrets are made to be revealed. The body's masks want to be torn away, hidden perversions want to be discovered, the causes of our suffering want to be brought to light. The eyes of the guardians of morals have always been focused on intimate facts. The border areas between nature and culture are covered by multiple taboos, as are those between life and death, madness and reason. Wherever it is a question of animal life, of the fusing of bodies, of the excesses of intoxication, of the organism's mortality, there the human being is a danger to the moral order. The collective moral code is directed against this danger. It marks the thresholds of shame and prohibition, and forces the untamed human animal into the cage of normality.

The gaze of the apostle of morality is blocked by the wall of secrecy. Shame and obduracy are in no way the result of repressed drives, of a merciless prohibition on speech that the moral authorities are supposed to have imposed. Pastoral theology, civil law, pedagogy, and medicine are instead agents of investigation and disclosure. They are not concerned with repression in the shadows of privacy but with the discovery of all details, the confession of indiscretions, the denunciation of offenses. The advocates of openness loudly condemn alleged hypocrisies, complain at length about supposed demands to keep silent, and report in great detail what is not supposed to be discussed. They tirelessly demand confessions and insist on the duties of erotic correctness. Love, intoxication, and death are surrounded by recommendations and prohibitions. Whether prudish or permissive, it is always the same indiscreet curiosity that wants to uncover strange and terrible vices.

The boundaries set by prohibitions vary. Over the centuries they have shifted repeatedly. Between periods of moral severity there have been short-term lapses into the paradise of free and easy informality. Liberal eras such as the late Renaissance, the Rococo, and the Postmodern alternate with phases of moral rigidity. Every age seeks a new mental equilibrium, a balance between revelation and concealment, between prudery and frankness. In addition, the domain of social shame is by no means homogeneous. Alongside regions of virtuousness there are areas of insouciance. Shame is unequally distributed between the bed and the bathroom, the brothel and the TV studio.

For centuries, nakedness was viewed as a moral disgrace and flesh was considered weak, infirm, and unclean. In cloisters, those earlier places for the exercise of discipline, the monks developed a way of life that was only later disseminated as a social standard. They slept in separate beds with a candle constantly burning at their sides, wore night-shirts, and went to great lengths to avoid exposing themselves while changing clothes. Nakedness elicited desire and degradation. It signified a withdrawal and exclusion from social life. A naked woman was the very embodiment of lust; a naked man was a wild barbarian, nearly a madman. Persons condemned to death had their clothes torn off when they went to the place of execution.

At the same time, people sometimes showed a certain lack of concern. In princely courts, a lady who revealed a naked calf was at times more shocking than one who revealed her breasts. Countless courtesy books and compendiums of gallantry sought to regulate embarrassing situations. People discussed good manners in the theater, disapproved of bathing naked, and debated the decorum of marriage ceremonies. The higher one stood on the social scale, the greater one's right to act shamelessly. The Sun King in Versailles was godlike also because, for him, there were no rules of decorum. He could show himself naked, hold audiences while sitting on the toilet, or change his shirt in front of everyone. Every private act was a state act. Noble ladies and gentlemen were allowed to receive lower-ranking persons while in their baths or on their toilets. In contrast, ordinary citizens had to completely conceal themselves. They were never allowed to appear undressed before a respectable person. It was not nakedness but rather masquerade that showed humility and respect.

In the bourgeois age shame took on a special moral significance. Self-censure anticipated social proscription. Manners hardened into morality. The new conscience, powerfully underpinned by the professional status of physicians and municipal hygiene officials, allowed a certain relaxation of criminal law. Vices, sins, and dishonorable acts went unpunished so long as they did not endanger society. Sexual offenses such as incest or sodomy were no longer subject to severe corporal punishment. Only the punishment for pedophilia was continually made harsher. The bourgeoisie opposed the cult of descendants to the noble cult of ancestors. The child was no longer merely a fetus and the bearer of the family name but was the heir to his father's property and ambitions.

The demi-monde of frivolity offered compensation for the inhibitions of everyday life. There ladies indulged in costly whims and cared for their delicate skins by bathing in milk, champagne, or strawberry juice. Little waves of pornography washed beneath the bastions of demure behavior. In ladies fashions, repressed eroticism remained alive in the corset, necklines fell, evening parties were enlivened by the emergence of Venus and her nymphs out of their foam, the glittering atmosphere of the Belle Époque produced the striptease, and, despite the scandals and show trials, the arts rediscovered nudity.

Today shamelessness seems finally to have firmly established itself. Nakedness hardly gives offense, and public talk about intimate matters is not embarrassing. In exchange for a fee and fleeting notoriety, people voluntarily allow millions of interested TV viewers to watch them perform all sorts of bodily activities. With cameras running, they present their private inclinations and preferences, even if these are only for a curious piece of jewelry or a conspicuous physical attribute. Round the clock, studio guests display the details of their private lives and discuss before the eyes of the nation every sort of triviality. The public is interested, because everyday life is far less liberal than the media and advertising suggest. The effort to conceal sexual intercourse from others is just as widespread as it has ever been. Even if more skin is shown, the line where shame begins has merely shifted. The visible body is largely de-sexualized, and in some cases even the genitals have lost their power to excite. Pious immigrants may consider Western culture to be shameless, but its inhabitants blush just as before, only not when they see naked bodies on the beach. The same person who regularly takes sun baths naked in public places turns off the lights at home when things get intimate.

∞

The greatest threats to the body's secrets are not people's self-revelations but rather government attacks on the organic foundations of society. The state marks out the spaces and times in which it distributes human bodies. It takes control over future life even before it is born. On the pretext of ethical oversight, it penetrates ever deeper into the flesh. In the control over abortions, the point is not at all to protect the unborn subject from medical or parental arbitrariness. Procreation, pregnancy, and offspring are public opportunities for bio-politics, which is constantly trying to do away with the privacy of the female body. Recently fertilization and cell growth have attracted the authorities' attention. The debate about embryos, bio-patents, and genetic testing has nothing to do with ethics. Ultimately it is the sovereign that decides when human life begins and when it ends. Behind the rhetoric of human dignity, a bureaucratic power is at work that seeks to control the production and supervision of the human organism. Sooner or later, an individual's genetic makeup will be used as a criterion for assigning rights to citizenship and benefits. For power based on law and order, however, the nightmare would be the cloning of individuals—though this is still very improbable in biotechnological terms. Surveillance cameras and police laboratories would be helpless to deal with a society of cloned doubles.

The authorities pursue a demographic policy and subsidize procreations when faced with a threat that the state's population might die out or that there might be a shortage of young civil servants. They use tax revenues paid by other citizens to encourage population growth or, if necessary, to impose birth control in overpopulated regions. Campaigns to promote hygiene, public health, and collective diets are all part of the program of the modern welfare state, along with conditioning the body and punishing drug and alcohol use. The authorities regulate sexual relations, enact prohibitions on sexual deviations, and impose penalties for vices. People who indulge in forbidden pleasures or take unusual risks must pay fines. Anyone who does not adhere to health regulations will be detected and unmasked. The modern state has inherited the clergy's task of looking after morals and producing virtuous individuals. Government also intervenes at the end of life. When a subject commits suicide, the state accepts this without imposing punishment. Every power reaches its limit when it encounters the human being's sovereignty over his own existence. But the citizen is denied help in dying or the right to a bearable death in accord with his own wishes. The goal is not a good life but rather survival at any price. It is as if power does not want to let its subjects go until their hearts stop. Only when a person's death promises to produce a greater utility is the final end point advanced. For harvesting transplantable organs, what matters is not cardiac death but brain death. In a state between life and death the body may be gutted. The sovereign proves his power by defining death. Someday internal organs will belong to the public authorities.

Once a regime was considered totalitarian if it occupied all areas of social life. Modern bio-power does not limit itself to controlling social relationships. It grasps humans as organic, living beings. Even before the first breath is drawn, bio-power seizes control over the body, granting and refusing the right to life. This soft, law-abiding totalitarianism destroys private existence in its physical center, in the inviolability of the body and human nature.

7 PRIVATE SPACES

The shell of the private protects us against the fear of nothingness. It promises endurance and survival. Its inner order seems assured. Here passions are tamed, here life can proceed peacefully. The private home is the site of social rootedness. Its inhabitants know where they belong, where they can stay. Here they are at home. But the domicile is also an economic and political fact. Domestic life is determined not only by love and togetherness but by power and money as well. The home is also a place of strife and rivalry. To found a family is to enclose a hearth that guarantees independence. But private space is also a kind of property, an object of investment, a heritage of stone, a realm for oneself where one is one's own master but a realm that still allows participation in the political public sphere. Without a fixed domicile, there is no right to vote.

The harmonious ideal of the cozy, secure home that many contemporaries still cling to was certainly indebted to a class privilege. Nineteenth-century bourgeois could build walls around their intimate households. They lived comfortably and owned property. Reception rooms were separated from the family refuge. Behind the front door lay the foyer. There visitors were stopped and evaluated. Anyone who had not been invited went no further. The family presented itself to guests in the dining room. At the dining table, business deals were made and marriages arranged. But family members also went to the dining room every day to chat with one another. When the meal was finished, the wife took up her knitting, the husband his newspaper, and the children their toys. The lady of the house received guests in the parlor, while the master of the house met friends and partners in the billiard room. Children were allowed to enter the parlor only when guests were there. Family photos had no place there. The parents' bedroom was strictly off limits to strangers. The kitchen was located in the furthest corner of the house. The smell of the kitchen sink, the drains, and the garbage can offended the nose. Before private bathrooms and water closets were introduced, many houses had only unheated corners where a chamber pot, a jug of water, and a bidet stood. The authorities often had to impose sewers and flush toilets by decree. Many a homeowners protested these attacks on their freedom as unsanitary. They preferred to live with dirty hands, put up with fetid odors, and keep their excrements private.

In striking contrast to the hierarchized private space of the bourgeois world were the miserable conditions under which the lower classes lived. Farmers dwelt for the most part in shabby huts with walls of clay, straw, or heather. These often had only one room that served not only as kitchen, bedroom, cellar, and storeroom but also as cow stall and barn. Supplies and tools were kept there. These huts could not accommodate many children. So young people had to find work or move away to earn their own livings. If hunger became too oppressive, many poor people sought salvation by running away. They moved to other rural areas or to cities, where often they were locked up.

Lower-class urban neighborhoods were seats of infection, overcrowded, poorly ventilated, and without running water. Many families lived in only one room. Along the walls stood the beds, a table, cupboards, a stand with a gas range; in one corner was the sewing machine, and in the opposite corner clotheslines were strung. Here people also shared their private spheres with other inhabitants. The walls separated the domestic area from society, but there was not enough room inside to reserve space for individuals. People did not sleep alone, and the slightest indisposition was immediately noticed. There was no room to have one's own corner. Thus, when among the family, one had to carry one's personal possessions in the pockets of trousers or jackets.

By withdrawing into their cozy homes, the bourgeois distanced themselves from the common people, separating their lives from the street and the lower classes. Only in the second half of the twentieth century did the majority of the population acquire more private space. Rooms became larger; intimacy was democratized. Even low-income housing projects had inside toilets and bathrooms. A private home in the suburbs, surrounded by a little garden and a fence, became accessible for many people. Nowadays it is not unusual for everyone to have his own room, even in lower-middle-class homes.

The cozy home was usually the collective space of a family or group sharing lodgings. There were good reasons to protect it. Only in an enclosed area could people pursue intimate relationships, express their feelings freely, and give themselves to each other. Only in a protected interior space could they lay aside the armaments of self-assertion and show their vulnerability. Family life is marked by love and commitment, respect and care, but also at times by ignorance, passion, and strife. In the cozy home, conflicts can become particularly acute when there are no third parties to mediate. The knowledge of another's weakness greatly increases the ability to inflict injury. Nonetheless, people can shape their intimate relationships the way that they want to only in a secure, protected space, free from meddling guardians of morality and unobserved by neighbors or officials.

∾

Along with group spaces there are refuges for intimacy reserved for the individual alone. In a common living space, personal atmospheres soon come into conflict. Even in the lap of the family, people are repelled by the smells of others. Shame at being seen by others increases the desire for distance and solitude. At first, the secluded garden served as a discreet place for amorous experiences and intimate companionship. The bedroom held not only the bed, that stage for conjugal passion and breeding ground for diabolical emanations, but also the private treasures—jewelry, books, folding screens, silverware. The study, kept under lock and key, was reserved for the master of the house. Children were not allowed to enter this sacred place. For reading, keeping books, and prayer, a table and chair were enough. But then the workroom also contained private collections—coins, medals, mugs. Later on, the home office was outfitted with writing implements and computers, and decorated with personal souvenirs, trophies, and pictures.

These rooms, along with the private apartments that are becoming increasingly common in large cities, have continued to provide private refuges. A room of one's own hides the individual from the eyes of his housemates. Like an apartment, it is a protected space for an unobserved life. There one need not feel that anyone is watching. A refuge allows one to temporarily opt out of society and find a place of peace and tranquility where one can indulge one's inclinations, lose oneself in one's thoughts, work out secret projects, care for one's body, or do nothing at all, without being urged by anyone to act, speak, or work.

In a refuge, we can determine for ourselves what objects we want around us. The interior is based on a monopoly of use. Personal things give the space an inconspicuous feeling of familiarity. Some objects are irreplaceable. Their market value might be small, but their personal significance is so great that damage to them would be experienced as a serious loss. The child's favorite toy, the adults' heirloom or family photo, the old chair, the chest of drawers—for years, even decades, these items have shaped our personal environment. Our bodies move among them with somnambulistic security. Even in the dark our hands know where things are, our body knows the distances and the passageways by heart. The body inhabits the room. Any unauthorized intrusion into this order of things damages our personal living sphere. The demand that the home be inviolable implies, first of all, that this familiar world with all its known rules and objects is protected. This demand is not contradicted when exhibitionists, fascinated by technology, use Web-cams to post pictures of their private spaces on the Internet. Some people try to supplement their incomes by providing private peep-shows, and others use the web to make personal contacts. By presenting their personal interior lives, they voluntarily deprive themselves of their places of refuge. To be sure, this blithe generosity presupposes the existence of a private space. The Web-cammer could reveal no other space to others' curiosity and lasciviousness. He remains free to decide when to turn his webcam on or off and whether he will illuminate every part of his refuge so that it all becomes visible. He alone ultimately decides how he shows himself to the public.

Houses, apartments, and rooms are stationary refuges. The automobile provides people with a vehicle that they can arrange as a private interior space. In this room on wheels they can escape domestic constraints and travel through the world without having to give up the security of the familiar. A car can take people where they want to go without regard to schedules or air routes. In this hollow space one moves freely and anonymously through the public sphere, at least so long as a traffic jam doesn't prevent one from doing so. These days, even mass-produced cars can be individually equipped. The colors of the fabrics, of paint, and the floor mats, wheels and rims, spoilers, chrome, decals, and electronic extras can be selected from a broad range of options. Radios and CD or MP3 players provide the desired background sound; telephones, laptop adapters, and navigation systems ensure that one can stay in contact even when far away. Slipcovers, lucky charms, or flowers over the dashboard; local emblems, advertising slogans, or political bumper stickers; crocheted pillows or stuffed animals in the back window—no matter how stereotypical the accessories may look, they personalize the vehicle's interior. The list of extras is so long that every individual can shape his own traveling room. A car is not only a means of self-representation in the battle for status and prestige but also a refuge for mobile intimacy. As a vehicle it is a public object; as a room it is a private object. Although it can be looked into from the outside, one can brush one's teeth undisturbed while waiting for the light to change, clean one's nose or ears, put on lipstick or comb one's hair. A conversation inside the car is not heard outside. Sometimes a car is also a substitute for one's bed at home, allowing one to take a nap or engage in erotic adventures.

∾

Private spaces are vulnerable in many ways. In addition to social attacks, material steps may also be taken that destroy the private sphere. Transparent architecture that does away with interior walls or replaces them with sheets of glass exposes our lives to others. In many cultures, boundary stones, doors, or lintels mark the transition from one world to another. "Crossing the threshold" means entering another area. Even if purification rituals are no longer in force, the threshold value of such transitions still survives in today's profane private world. Knocking on a door and requesting permission to enter is not simply a matter of conventional politeness. This gesture also testifies to a sense of spatial differences. It is destroyed when doors are removed and everyone has free access to every space, including the bathroom and the bedroom. Disregarding transitions also means disregarding personal areas of shame. The culture of openness, which would like to lift all private barriers, is a brutal intrusion on the personal sphere. Open houses and rooms presuppose a culture of respect and discretion that ensures that doors are considered closed even when they do not exist, and that shades need not be pulled down because every passerby is able to curb his curiosity.

If doors are locked, technical help is required to penetrate into private spaces. Keyholes offer narrowly limited views and poor sound quality. Listening devices and bugs thus continue to be the most important instruments of acoustic surveillance. They are used not only by the police, intelligence services, and drug-control officials but also by private detectives, jealous husbands, suspicious business partners, fearful parents, and troublesome voyeurs. Such devices have now been so miniaturized that they are almost impossible to detect. A camera that can be seen gives people a feeling that they are being watched, even if it has secretly been turned off. Mini-microphones are virtually invisible. The person concerned does not know whether someone is listening in. The camera's eye forces people to be circumspect, whereas bugs, because they are imperceptible, lead people to speak frankly.

Listening devices must be brought to the site. Someone has to come up with a pretext for entering in order to place the bug in an olive in the martini glass. With new directional microphones and laser technology, this risk need no longer be taken. A laser beam can be focused on a window from a considerable distance. Sounds in the room cause the windowpane to vibrate, and the device records these vibrations with great precision. Noise can easily be filtered out digitally so that the suspicious conversation is clearly heard. Even loud music or toilet flushing cannot provide a defense against this kind of eavesdropping.

Bugs are interested in sounds and conversations, video cameras in actions and movements. The video camera, that universal modern observational device, serves not only to attack private space but also to defend it. Mounted on external façades, driveways, and front gates, on garages, parking areas, or backyards, it keeps an eye on the approaches. The monitors at points of entry are not only supposed to provide early warning by recognizing dangers and recording suspicious figures, but also and especially to frighten away petitioners, thieves, and vandals and prevent them from entering the private sphere. But they make even harmless visitors feel like unauthorized intruders. Like the familiar peephole in the apartment door, the video camera allows a surreptitious view of the corridor, the entrance, the gate outside. Anyone at those places must expect to be seen before he has even introduced himself. While he is adjusting his hair, straightening his tie, smoothing his crumpled jacket, and putting on a friendly visitor's face, the eyes of the mistrustful person inside are already on him. One must therefore already have prepared one's appearance before approaching the threshold.

Not only the border areas but also the inner rooms of the private fortress are under observation. Concerned parents install video cameras in yards and children's rooms or hide nanny-cams in toys so they can keep an eye on their children and their children's nursemaids. They put GPS tracking bracelets on their kids so they can't leave the property, or they set up a baby monitor so they can immediately react to unusual noises in the baby's room. Sometimes even semiprivate spaces like kindergartens and preschools are equipped with video cameras, allowing parents to see their children "live." Most of these parents are just curious to see how their kids behave when they are not there. They are driven above all by a demand for absolute certainty. They can't bear their offspring not being under parental protection. This technology is not meant to help strangers spy on strangers. It is there only to keep an eye on one's own family. The children don't know they are being monitored, and the teachers don't tell their charges what the little boxes on the ceiling or the glass eye in the clown's head are really there for.

∾

In Western countries founded on the rule of law, surveillance of private spaces is regulated. Out of respect for the private sphere, laws prohibit listening in on telephone conversations and filming others without their knowledge. At the same time, a frightened and therefore repressive public demands investigations targeting potential offenders, suspected traitors, organized syndicates, and terrorist networks. In spectacular cases of rape, depravity, or child abuse, the public castigates the neighbors' silence and the officials' failure to take action. The grounds for legal observation are manifold. Crime has many different faces, and the number of its possible victims is unlimited.

In some countries children are considered full-fledged, if defenseless, citizens who need special protection. The family is no longer solely responsible for its progeny. State and society have themselves undertaken to determine how children are brought up and to see to it that the weak come to no harm. Any sexual attack, any domestic abuse or violence, confirms this claim and destroys the freedom of the sacred family. When love is gone, the law steps in. The judicial system is responsible for ensuring the welfare of women and children, the sharing of income, and the regulation of contact during a family cease-fire. It does not always force its way into the bedroom and the children's room on its own initiative. Attentive neighbors report to the police the shouting and screaming they hear going on next door. Teachers, doctors, and nursery-school personnel urge officials to question self-willed or injured children, and ultimately married couples sometimes call upon the courts to set visiting or custodial rights or to record sexual indiscretions in their files. Not only do state agencies make use of the tendency to regulate everything by shining a light into the space of the family; welfare monitors and informers, even individual family members, also urge the lifting of private barriers.

The prosecution of crimes is always accompanied by the documentation of private contacts. This includes surveillance of private homes. If someone's domicile cannot be spied upon from within, whether for lack of legal authorization or because one is dealing with conspirators who are on the lookout for listening devices, one has to resort to watching the entrances. All day investigators watch the doors and windows to see who comes and goes.

This "traffic analysis" can, however, provide no more than indirect evidence. It can only determine who came into contact with whom and at what time. What goes on behind the windows escapes observation.

Buildings may be legally searched in cases of imminent danger or after obtaining a court order. Detectives enter private spaces, search closets and drawers, open doors, look in all the nooks and crannies. When searching for evidence, they show little respect. Personal items are carelessly thrown aside, papers and private notes are confiscated. The investigators respect no taboos. They turn every piece of laundry inside out, open every drawer, examine every piece of paper. Even if all the formal requirements have been met and a criminal offense is actually discovered, such a search leaves innocent friends and relatives with deep feelings of insecurity. The search is experienced as an assault, an inroad, not only because one has fallen under suspicion but also because one is suddenly forced to look on helplessly as foreign intruders occupy the world in which one had felt securely established and turn it upside down.

Secret searches are carried out without the occupants' knowledge. People are commonly arrested in police states and held in custody long enough for others to rummage through their homes while they are interrogated about some trivial event. In countries based on the rule of law, covert searches are also possible by means of electronic technology. Trojan horses, insidious spy programs that attach themselves to a person's e-mail program, give government investigators access to private computers without the target ever noticing.

Covert trespassing is another way to intentionally wear down dissidents. While the target is traveling or out shopping, spies break into his home and make two tiny changes; they move a pair of glasses from the desk to the piano, shift a knickknack a few inches away from its usual location. When the person returns home, at first he doesn't notice anything. Then he looks for his glasses and is surprised that they are not on the desk where he thought he left them. A few days later he notices that the little knickknack is not exactly where it used to be. He is puzzled and wonders what is going on. When such things happen repeatedly, a vague disquiet begins to grow inside him, a fear that is difficult to suppress. The victim wonders if he is going mad, and then gradually suspects that *they* have been in his home and might reappear at any time.

The most brutal attack on private space is a raid. It, too, is part of the arsenal of the politics of terror. The area is blocked off, and the inhabitants find themselves trapped. Street by street, building by building, room by room, everything is combed through. The searchers demolish anything that stands in their way, wantonly destroying what the inhabitants cherish and value. This temporary erasure of everything private is immediately intimidating. People are no longer masters in their own homes. The belief in the inviolability of the person, his home, and his property is abruptly swept away. Shouts and roars, abuse and scornful laughter, echo through the space. Knowing they have the upper hand, the investigators take pleasure in acting arbitrarily. They let some people go and attack others because they protest. Interrogations, endless checking, and hasty arrests are carried out on the spot.

Powerless rage overcomes many victims. Loud protests are pointless. Without warning, an alien, overwhelming force has thrust itself into, and fully occupied, one's area of life. The operation is often carried out summarily and without respect for the person involved. Anyone who looks suspect is thoroughly searched and arrested if any evidence of wrongdoing is found. Even if those arrested return safe and sound, they find their life refuges ransacked. The protective aura of privacy is destroyed.

8 PROPERTY

Private property does not have a good reputation. Although everyone tries to acquire it, it is considered objectionable. Someone who has many times more than the average level of resources cannot have come by them legitimately. Anything not earned by honest labor arouses suspicion and resentment. Money corrupts character, according to the proverb, and a lot of money corrupts it completely. Property is said to encourage the lower instincts: envy and miserliness, greed and vanity. No one can be rich and at the same time good and virtuous. Interest, capital, profit, even speculation—these elementary economic facts are suspect for many contemporaries. Campaigns against wealthy idlers, managers with princely salaries, or coldly calculating investors are generally applauded. Such people count on a society's moral economy, whose standards are far too traditional to deal with today's capitalism. So far as business is concerned, morals have seldom been up to date.

Attacks on property have always been a predilection among clerics, intellectuals, and agitators. In battling for power, someone who possesses nothing more than his belief, a mission, or a little bit of culture has to morally deprecate the other side. In the name of achievement and service, the

middle classes used to criticize the leisure and honor of the
aristocracy. The intellectual leaders of the lower classes in-
veighed against property and capital, and praised labor and
education. Although today everyone recognizes the advantages of mass consumption, the old resentments continue
to operate. Since property and wealth are still unequally
distributed, old popular slogans can still be used.

Private property is blamed for countless evils in our world:
for wars and competition, for poverty, exploitation, and
moral decline. Striving for profit is said to be unworthy and
damaging to community spirit. The sole virtue a business-
man is supposed to be capable of is honesty; he can never
attain the warm-heartedness of solidarity. Charging interest is usury, property is theft, capital is robbery, speculation
is fraud; wealth, that is, can be acquired and increased only
by crooked means. The expropriation of farmers, the exploitation of wage-slaves, unearned inheritances—all such
acquisition of property has always been considered unjust
and dubious. Private property is presumed to corrupt social morality. Property feeds selfishness. Private capital is
irresponsible, because owners can do what they want with
their property. Private property imposes no duties. It can
be increased or squandered, given away or concealed. No
one can tell the property owner what he must do with his
resources. For that reason, according to most, the state
should heavily tax large inheritances, fortunes, compensation, and so-called excess profits, manage currency rates,
and drive all speculators out of the country.

∾

The Fall, according to an old fable, occurred with the act
of appropriating land. The first man who fenced in a piece

of land founded the society of property. Others were naïve enough to imitate him. Instead of pulling out the fence stakes and filling in the ditches, everyone enjoyed his own fruits. But from that moment on, there was a division of labor and people needed one another's help. As soon as someone noticed that it was useful to lay aside enough supplies for two people, the original equality disappeared. Thus property was established, and the inequality of talents intensified oppositions. The stronger did more work, the more talented benefited more from their efforts, the cleverer found ways to complete work more quickly, and even when people did the same amount of work, some earned a great deal whereas others, even working themselves almost to death, earned very little.

Thus inequality among men did not result from ambition, fraud, or robbery but rather from the division of labor, the specialization of abilities, and the independence of one person's achievements from those of others. Inequality arose behind people's backs, so to speak, and was ultimately codified in laws. There can be no injustice when there is no property. But it also seems that there can be no justice when there is property. In order to give each individual his own, each must already have something. Anyone who has nothing deserves nothing, according to the principle of just compensation.

Property, allegedly, also divides men from one another. The exclusive right to use something excludes others. The borderline between mine and thine splits the community, destroys equality, and throws the individual into the ice-cold waters of the society of exchange, where many people enjoy credit but none enjoys trust, because each supposedly becomes a means to someone else's end.

Common life is no longer determined by the natural impulse to help one another, affection, and sympathy, but rather by egoistic feelings of vanity, rivalry, and hostility. The private individual is always out to expand his profits at the expense of others. In order not to go under himself, he has to surpass his rivals. Thus he is consumed by the ambition to increase his wealth; he is driven by a secret envy, a dark inclination to harm others. The richer a person becomes, the greater his avarice. Property transforms community into a society of lone wolves.

Very little of all this is true. No one is what he possesses. Vice and virtue correspond neither to the size of one's bank account nor to the extent of one's land holdings. People who have nothing are not automatically morally superior simply because they have less than they need. The battle for recognition, the will to power, the desire for fame, arrogance, and other negative qualities are completely independent from the institution of property. Nor are the feelings of positive mutuality, love, empathy, and trust based on material possessions. One does not have to be poor in order to be generous. True, without property there is no greed or envy, but there is also no giving and no liberality. Brotherliness presupposes private property. Someone who has nothing can share nothing. Even if the equality of goods were guaranteed, the causes of human quarrels would not be eliminated. Nowhere is there as much strife as among brothers. Anyone who only has what everyone has, has too little of many things. And he has too much of what he neither wants nor needs. Equality and common property do not ensure that basic needs will be peacefully met.

In any case, a society would quickly come to an end if its survival depended on the virtues of its citizens. A community that counts primarily on self-interest does not have to make high moral claims. It is content with average characters. The private property owner's market gets along without higher values. Exchange values are quite enough. To be sure, without property there would be no theft, no fraud, and no robbery. But so long as goods are in short supply, private distribution provides clear relationships. Everyone knows what belongs to him and what does not.

Property regulates not only relationships among things but also relationships among people. Property is social relationship mediated by relationships among things. Robinson Crusoe would never have had to meditate on his right to the treasures of his island had he been certain that no one else would ever turn up there. Without his man Friday, he would have had no property rights to the island, because he had no rights at all. No one can have a right for himself alone. Duties and claims exist only in relation to others. Property establishes exclusiveness among several individuals. The property owner alone has the right to make use of his property. He has despotic power over the things that belong to him. All other inhabitants of the world are excluded from them. In this way, property constitutes a special sphere of the private, on which no one else has any claim and which is not transparent to the public at large.

The separation of mine from thine creates social order. A peaceful society requires a clear allocation of goods. Hence their public use must be subject to general rules. This may be associated with personal severity or benefits.

But binding rules regarding property are indispensable. Clear property relationships ensure security. Otherwise each person could appropriate whatever he liked, independent of whether another person already had the use of it. No enjoyment would ever be certain. If the individual's property were not protected, he could never be sure of having shoes or clothing, food or housing.

Binding rules prevent conflicts. Law compensates for a lack of virtue. It imposes penalties for violations of the rules—penalties that the offender finds too high a price to pay for the advantages he could derive from his offense. Law protects the property owner, but it also ensures that property is not used to the disadvantage of others. One individual's right to free disposal ends at the point where another person's life is endangered or his freedom curtailed. As always, the final goal of property law is to protect each individual's freedom.

Law defines the legality of ownership. But it is based first of all on the legitimacy of acquisition. Property is acquired through appropriation or labor, through inheritance or voluntary transfer. Whether the distribution of property is just depends on how it was acquired, and not on how goods ought to be distributed. The justice of property is a historical question. Anyone who at some earlier time had a legitimate right to a certain good continues to have a right to it at the present time. Anyone who acquired his property through fraud, theft, or enslavement, who deprived other people of the fruits of their labor, caused them to live in accord with his will, or used force to prevent them from competing in trade, his property is not currently justified. Past misdeeds do not justify any present ownership. On the contrary, they require correction. For this reason it is right and proper that the victims of illegitimate expropriation should be able to demand, even decades later, that their property be returned to them. And therefore justice requires that people who were compelled to do forced labor be given a concrete compensation above and beyond the symbolic recognition of the harm done them. Injustices need to be set right on the basis of what would have happened had the injustice not taken place when it did.

∾

Property gives rise to social intercourse. Far from estranging people from one another, it creates new bonds. Society begins with exchange among strangers. When one person is selling something that another desires, and the latter pays what the former asks for it, people meet who would otherwise never become acquainted with each other. Competition, so often reviled, drives rivals to court prospective buyers. In the end, the winner is the one who understands the buyer's secret wishes even before he knows he has them. In a free market, people can develop their peculiarities and needs to a far greater extent than in the stifling warmth of the community. Among the countless private property owners there is always one who wants to sell something he doesn't need. If everyone had the same things, then everyone would have to be content with what he had. Not even in their wishes could people distinguish themselves from one another.

Exchange among private individuals is the basis for equality and freedom. Trading partners recognize each other as equals. Each accepts the other as a subject with his own will. The sales contract that they agree to does not establish equality of status or property but rather a voluntary relationship between peers. We should not expect more from a society that shields people from the pressure of the community and is supposed to put a protective distance between them.

An equal distribution of possessions is not only hopeless but would be disastrous. Differences in skill, care, and diligence would immediately break through any kind of equality. Worse yet, in the name of equality, development of these virtues would have to cease, thus forcing society back to a meager level. Instead of preventing a few people from falling into poverty and begging, the survival of the whole society would be at stake. To promptly block any new inequality, all property owners would have to be constantly monitored. Everyone would have to reveal what he had. Any surplus would have to be immediately taken away, every secret treasure discovered and confiscated. The craving for equality leads directly to tyranny. It is true that absolute equality can do without any further observation. No one would have anything that anyone else could still covet. But a policy of equality that went to any length to rid people of a sense of differences would also destroy, along with privacy, any kind of motivation.

The abolition of property would reduce the individual to a public figure. In property, the individual will achieves objective reality. The power of disposal over things that belong only to oneself marks out one's place in the world. It creates a sphere to which no one else is allowed access, a safe realm of action in which the individual can experience the effectiveness of his acts and develop self-confidence. Not having any property means having no settled place. By limiting citizens to an objective relationship mediated by property, society releases the individual as a person.

A have-not often loses his political protection. He becomes an outsider. In contrast, property opens up new possibilities. Since the abolition of the poll tax as a criterion of voting rights, everyone can participate in public occasions, but it is still easier to do so if one is economically independent. Only if one has control over one's own necessities of life, if one has moved a certain distance beyond the pressure of drudgery and has acquired the freedom to occasionally indulge in leisure, can one actively enter the political world.

Private property also means freedom from necessity, from the coerced existence of slaves to labor, and it is the presupposition of the transformation of *Animal laborans* into *Homo politicus*. Property provides a material foundation for the fortress of privacy. The individual can keep society at arm's length. Through mutual recognition of property, citizens guarantee their private spheres. They agree that property remains beyond the reach of the eyes and ears of the public. A people that does not recognize property lacks a sense for freedom. There is no personal freedom without the political guarantee of private property, and there is no independence of lifestyles, of opinions and action, without a minimum of economic independence.

∾

In human life, only two things are certain: death and taxes. In the case of an emergency, the state decides whether to take a citizen's life; usually it takes his property. The amount and frequency of taxes was once determined by the frequency of wars. Every new military campaign required a full treasury. But princes commonly were content to levy a tenth of a person's income and of his goods and chattels. Today, subjects work half their lives for public institutions. They no longer pay for a landlord's court, dynastic wars, or campaigns of colonial conquest; instead, they pay for the organization of their own lives.

Modern states have long been managed in function of expenditures. The nationalization of private property necessarily follows from the growth of state expenditures. Tax authorities still base all their calculations on increasing state revenues rather than on reducing benefits. Not saving, but distributing and wasting is their motto. For centuries, societies got along without centralized state direction. Now, however, the slightest problem automatically elicits a call for government aid. Citizens' demands and the growth of contributions and taxes mutually determine each other. Desires grow along with expenditures. The state takes from the citizen what the citizen demands of it. But the services for which taxes are supposed to pay are often not forthcoming.

Taxes are payments made without implying a specific service in return. The purpose for which they will be used is left open. This distinguishes taxes from insurance premiums or fees for services or licenses. Just as the taxpayer does not have a claim to a service of equal value, so the state does not have the right to levy taxes for a specific project. An energy tax for the purpose of reducing labor costs or a property tax for raising the level of education would contradict the basic principle of taxation. Taxes are never connected with a particular purpose, or indeed with any purpose whatever. Politicians can make free use of the money in the government's treasury. Taxes are not reserved for the provision of protection and security, that single legitimate, core task of the state.

The state's raison d'être is not to provide welfare but rather to guarantee rights to protection and freedom that shield the individual from encroachments by others. Only violation of the law requires a political power that goes beyond the individual's power of action. Protection against war and crime is the state's primary task, and only this task justifies a budget financed by taxes. Present-day state financing has moved far away from this basic principle. The state has taken over so many functions from society that, for most contemporaries, it is no longer conceivable that aid, care, and prohibitions could even exist without state support. It suffices to announce a political intention in order to conceal what taxes really are: an arbitrary act, a contribution without equivalent, and an inexhaustible resource for state power through which the latter finances itself.

The arbitrary nature of tax systems can be seen by a glance at the facts. No limits have ever been set to the tax collectors' greed. No economic activity proceeds without charge, whether it involves buying flowers, repairing a washing machine, or purchasing land. Having a dog is taxed, as is gasoline, natural gas, tobacco, or liquor. Taxes are withheld from salaries, income is squeezed, profits skimmed. The state, however, cannot prevent its citizens from being lucky. In many countries, lottery winnings and prize monies are subject to taxation, as are inheritances, gifts, and money won at the slot machines. Not even protection against bad luck, in the form of life and property insurance, is safe from the government's clutches. What one has earned and owns, the use and consumption of goods— everything is taxable. Whatever the citizen does, he must constantly make co-payments to the tax authorities.

The concept of the total state does not mean that social life alone is monitored; economic activities are also under surveillance. There is the transparency of transactions, fiscal and social authorities' access to all bank accounts and deposits, the registration of currency transactions and transfers of funds to foreign countries, the lifting of banking secrecy, and so on. Only the completely transparent bank customer corresponds to the state's ancient dream of being fully informed about its subjects' property, in order to be able to attack it directly in case of an emergency. The search for hidden treasures is among the chief activities of customs agents and investigators. As emigration is often denounced as a betrayal of the nation, so the idea of a tax on funds transferred abroad is in accord with a policy of national protection. Unpatriotic individuals who leave the tax territory forever are supposed to leave behind at the border everything they have legally earned over the years through trade, purchase, labor, or gifts. Only the poor and those without property are allowed to turn their backs on the sacred nation-state without being harassed.

A sovereign is someone who can daily demand with impunity that his subjects pay up. Since time immemorial, tax rates have been a criterion of sovereignty. No state exists without the obligation to pay taxes. Even before the duty to perform military service and attend school, the common duty to pay taxes is the foundation of modern state power. Now that the privileges of the nobility and the clergy have been abolished, no one is immune to taxation. The idea of fiscal justice requires that everyone must be equal before the taxman. That, however, in no way guarantees that justice will be done. Only if welfare tax payments and the state benefits provided in return were equal would there be true justice. In reality, however, not a few state benefits are superfluous, too expensive, or ineffective. The tax receiver clearly has the advantage. Coerced taxation is the freedom of states. What the citizen loses in property, the state gains in the resources at its disposal.

Taxes are in no sense of general utility. The state regularly fails to fulfill its duties. It cannot guarantee peace or security. It does not protect citizens against economic need, can produce neither work nor economic growth, and in many places allows roads and education to decay. The yearly list of cases of waste and mismanagement only mentions the obvious ones. The sole "benefit" taxpayers can be sure to receive is the growth of the state bureaucracy and centers of para-governmental control and regulation. After all, the power elites must provide offices and sinecures for their clienteles and party faithful. They use taxes to finance government employees, the army, and public services. Taxes nourish bureaucratic domination.

However, all sorts of believers in the state consider taxes a just demand. For them, the state is the central distributive organ, an institution for mutual plundering. Taxation is based on the idea that everyone can live at the expense of everyone else. That is why politics concentrates

primarily on the problem of determining who should receive certain goods. However, free disposal over property
implies first of all the freedom to give things away voluntarily. The state as distributor determines who may receive
welfare benefits or an inheritance, not whether there is
a right to give or bequeath something to someone without taxation. It limits itself to ensuring a just distribution
among the receivers and disregards the freedom to transfer, to donate, to give. In a free society, however, what
counts is not the distribution of goods but rather their fair
exchange, not taking at others' expense but rather giving
of one's own free will.

Every year, the faithful subject works several months
without pay for the state bureaucracy. This amounts to
involuntary labor. The taxation of earned income is therefore a kind of concealed forced labor. Although slave owners' overseers and bloodhounds cannot force people to
work, a nontransparent system of management that immediately withholds part of salaries for the public treasury
and for obligatory insurance can. The state does not work
for its subjects; the latter work for the state. It purloins
salaries and work time. If the fruit of someone's labor is
taken from him, it is the same as if he were deprived of
hours, days, even months of his life. A program of open-
ended obligatory labor for the unemployed or young, as is
sometimes demanded, would only further extend a struc-
tural principle that has long since been implemented in
the form of the general taxation of labor. If an individual
works without pay for others, then the latter determine,
independently of the person's will, what he must do and
to which ends he must work. In this way they become the

beneficiaries of his labor. Through forced labor, the state acquires a right of disposal over its subjects. The individual no longer has a monopoly of control over himself. He can escape such relationships only if he works unofficially, on the side, and does not declare his income. A shadow economy has long since spread that allows people to work not for others but for themselves alone.

9   INFORMATION

There are only a few places in society where one can feel free from the observation of strangers. People are constantly sizing one another up. They want to know what others have in mind, where they are going, what they are thinking, how they see themselves and others. Even if they don't exchange a word, even if in restaurants, train compartments, or waiting rooms, everyone stays in his own place, people watch each other out of the corners of their eyes. They monitor their environments in order to recognize dangers in time. No one should suddenly come too close. Even if nothing happens, they need to be assured that everything is all right.

This changes as soon as misunderstandings or conflicts of interest arise. Relaxed attentiveness becomes mistrust. In a conflict, people can be deceived, cheated, betrayed. Since no one can know what someone else knows, the latter remains an inexhaustible source of uncertainty. In the daily battle for money, love, power, and recognition, a person who has discovered more about others than they have discovered about him has the advantage. The unequal distribution of knowledge produces a continual stream of information that an individual cannot possibly control. Others commonly know more about him than he would like. And often enough he knows too little about them in order to get a head start on them. Thus there is only one way out: since it costs more to discover others' secrets than to keep one's own, we make use of a deliberate information politics.

Every self-representation treads the narrow line between publicity and privacy, between conformism and stubborn independence. If all people presented themselves as unique beings, as eccentric loners who have nothing in common with others, then society would be a collection of strange figures whose knowledge of one another was limited to what each showed on the outside. The social context would disintegrate into an abrupt series of brief contacts. If, conversely, everyone simply met others' expectations of them, then society would degenerate into a forum for opportunists without character. No one could be relied upon. Someone who says yes to everything shows himself to be a man without qualities. From one minute to the next, he changes his convictions, preferences, and interests. Notorious conformists are people without obstinacy, without inner substance. They echo what others say and agree with everyone. They have no opinions and no memory; indeed, they seem not even to have a relationship with themselves. Self-presentation is therefore the art of not seeming to be like everyone else, but also not like anyone else at all.

An individual's personal information politics disseminates the data about himself that he wants to be in circulation. The most inconspicuous staging consists in concealing one's existence. False passports, assumed names, falsified birth certificates, dyed hair, false beards, sunglasses, retouched photos or fingerprints—these serve solely to allow someone to disappear behind a mask. Such props are used not only by spies, thieves, smugglers, and actors but also by ex-cons, call girls, minors who want to see an X-rated film, and asylum seekers telling the authorities some wild tale. Professional observers, covert investigators, or curious kings who mix incognito with their subjects also conceal their identities. They all manipulate documents and disguise themselves so as not to be recognized.

A favorite variant is leading a double life. The individual moves in two separate social groups. No one must notice that he has a second life. A wife has an affair, regularly meets her lover in a small apartment rented for the purpose, visits carefully chosen places with him, and acts as if she were not married and was busy with her work. At home, she leads an inconspicuous family life, meets relatives and friends, takes care of her children and husband, and explains her regular absences as unavoidable business trips and professional obligations. In both contexts, she uses the same legend to keep her other life secret. No one knows her as a whole person. The greatest risk run by this double life is inadvertent revelation. Both social groups must remain strictly separate from each other. A note left on the chest of drawers, a telephone call, an acquaintance who happens to have seen the lovebirds in another part of the city—and the cover is blown.

Self-representations not only tell us who someone is. They also conceal his intentions, thoughts, or feelings. Staging one's own inner life is a particularly delicate task. Great acting ability is required to restyle involuntary gestures into consciously willed ones. As a rule, people reveal more than they can control. Everyday blunders, slips of the tongue, embarrassments, and memory lapses, grimaces and involuntary body language, folded arms or crossed legs, changes in one's tone of voice, a thoughtless word—the experienced observer always discerns more than the person representing himself wants him to. In conversation, people betray thoughts about which they haven't said a word, and long practice and concentration are required to keep track of all our life signs. An anxious effort to control oneself already attracts the observer's attention. He pricks up his ears, keeps a sharp eye out for the unspoken, curiously probes for hidden meanings. Ultimately the only protection against discrediting oneself lies in merciful inattention on the part of the observer. Slips, ambiguities, and errors may be ignored so long as no one is directly harmed by them.

The individual finds support when he can confide his secrets to a third party. People who are in on the secrets are expected to keep them to themselves. Discretion was long demanded by the institution of professional confidentiality. Physicians were expected not to communicate information regarding a patient's illness. Bankers had to keep silent about their customers' transactions. Priests had to respect the secrecy of the confessional, and lawyers were forbidden to reveal anything that would undermine their clients' claims of innocence. A person who has been told another's secret makes it his own. He not only has to pretend to be ignorant of what the other person has involuntarily shown him, but he also must follow an old principle regarding third parties: he may make known neither what has not been expressly revealed nor what has been intentionally concealed.

Information politics guides the social distribution of knowledge. It separates the data that are to be accessible to everyone from those that must be reserved for initiates. Unlike spaces or things, information is not bound to material substrates. The exclusiveness of a private secret is therefore much more difficult to defend than a piece of land or a private room. Once something has become known, it can never again be concealed. Knowledge spreads in an instant, moves from mouth to mouth, is printed here and there. It is nearly impossible for an individual to correct false reports or unauthorized pictures. Neither court orders nor claims that accusations are groundless can restore a damaged reputation. What has once been ruined remains ruined forever.

༃

The reserve of information is first endangered by individual persons. Secrets known to more than one person are not secrets. Anyone who knows them can turn traitor and use them to extort hush money. The traitor communicates to third parties information that was entrusted to him under the seal of secrecy. He uses his knowledge to his own advantage. The payment he demands may be made in recognition, praise, or cash. Unlike a gossip who can keep nothing to himself, the traitor calculates costs and benefits. The benefit to be gained by betrayal seems to him worth the cost of losing a friendship. He silently cancels the relationship of trust. Whereas the person betrayed thinks his ally is reliable, the traitor has long since changed sides. At the appointed time he opens the gates of the fortress of privacy and lets in the forces besieging it.

Cold-blooded selfishness, however, can prove to be short-sighted. With the reward before his eyes, the traitor often ignores the consequences of his offense. Hardly has he handed over the document, transferred the computer file, or opened the door than he is paid—and rejected—by the receiver. Once he has communicated the information he has lost all value. He finds himself empty-handed between two stools, and the best thing he can do is quickly leave the social group. His reputation is spoiled once and for all. A person who changes sides must write off his previous existence. A traitor is never forgiven. Someone who has betrayed one person will betray another as well. Therefore, traitors generally try to hush up any indication of what they have done. Although it is a common way of communicating social information, betrayal always smells of a personal lack of fidelity and honor.

Denunciation is a special case of betrayal. It communicates information regarding the family or tribe, the circle of neighbors, colleagues, co-religionists, or fellow party members to their persecutors. The informer usually moves unnoticed among his victims but sometimes also acts as a spokesman for dissent in order to lead like-minded people to make careless remarks. He takes part in the discussions of opposition groups, keeps his ears open in the workplace, seeks contact with other people living in his building, and at the family dinner table stores in his memory everything a guest has said. In the long run, however, the spy can do his work only by leading a double life. He depends on his victim's not knowing what he is about. So long as the victim trusts him, the traitor learns something. And only so long as he has something to report does headquarters stand behind him. At the first hint of suspicion, the person under investigation may take countermeasures. He reveals false information and limits dangerous conversations to the closest circle of friends. Thus the spy is surprised by the suddenly innocuous nature of the conversations and has no idea that the others have long since figured out what he is doing.

Informers serve as intermediaries. Voyeurs keep everything to themselves. They spy for their own purposes. The voyeur is also an illegal collector of private information, but his motive is neither ideological nor commercial. Lust and curiosity drive him to peep over the windowsill or through the keyhole. He is interested not only in sexual activities but also in letters, conversations, daily routines, and hard drives. Some voyeurs are driven by a pure desire to watch, others by the excitement of violating a taboo, and still others by the secret conquest of someone else's private sphere. Voyeurs and hackers are not always interested in harming their victims. They often derive pleasure from leaving everything just as it is. The voyeur is there, leaves and comes again, without the victim realizing it. His unnoticed presence in another person's life is enough to satisfy him. Without being seen himself, he squeezes right up to someone. The voyeur leads a secret existence but is able to look into the most intimate areas. He sees what is hidden from everyone else. The conquest of forbidden zones is his triumph.

Among the achievements of civilization is that people don't want to know certain things about others. If one

nonetheless has learned something, it is considered fit-
ting to act as if one knew nothing about it and keep one's
private knowledge to oneself. We protect the privacy of
our friends by not gossiping about them. However, this
kind of restraint is becoming increasingly rare. Indiscretion is viewed almost as a democratic virtue because it
claims to treat everyone equally. Intrusiveness is connected with a striking inability to make meaningful dis-
tinctions between people. It levels out social differences
by destroying any kind of distance. Just as an assault on
one's standard of living is experienced as violence done to
one's person and as an attack on one's private sphere, so
indiscretion damages a person's inner reserve.

A favorite pastime of the social animal is gossiping.
Talking about third parties is a major source of entertain-
ment. It varies the monotony of everyday life by means
of dramatic, sad, but also exciting or absurd stories. Together, people can complain about others with impunity,
laugh about their weaknesses, or bemoan their fates. Outsiders can be depreciated and insiders praised. Through
gossip, the latest news is exchanged, rumors are spread,
and people get excited and laugh together. Schadenfreude
has always been the lowest form of human sociability.

Gossip is not concerned with truth. People share common prejudices and spin out their common fantasies.
Malicious gossip cares nothing for facts. It draws its nour-
ishment chiefly from slanders, rumors, and caricatures.
Rumors are spread not by eyewitnesses but by earwit-
nesses. "Have you already heard?" "Just imagine that!"
That is how such tales usually begin. People whisper together, gesticulate, make spiteful remarks, complement

and confirm one another. The limits imposed by discretion are lifted. Gossip communicates information that was never intended for strangers' ears.

Gossip has diverse functions. It evens out differences in information among members of the group and thereby strengthens internal bonds. Private reports regarding third parties are combined into a collective knowledge, an open secret that holds the group together. Through their excitement over indecencies, chatterboxes and gossips mutually confirm their sense of their own uprightness. The gossiping group feels that it is a community of the righteous. At the same time, defamatory gossip is a weapon of social distinction. The uninitiated and the suspect remain excluded. Gossip is nothing other than casual conversation at the expense of others. It confers rank, reputation, and status, and thereby determines the dividing line between initiates and outsiders.

∿

As a form of sociability, gossip is usually confined to a person's immediate environment—to his relatives, his colleagues at work, the neighborhood. The function of personal information for public institutions is entirely different from its function for private ones. Information is the central source of power for the modern bureaucratic state. Without data regarding labor, income, and wealth there can be no taxation, no insurance system, and no public welfare. Without information there is no internal or external security, no protection against crime or foreign invaders. The security state is based on controlling its subjects and on the transparency of living conditions. The wider the scope of its tasks, the less the value accorded the private sphere. The obligation to attend school, pay taxes, and do military service, as well as care and welfare, would not be conceivable if information about subjects were not on file and in data banks.

With the transition from summary equality to individual justice, the bureaucracy's need for information has rapidly increased. When no one is supposed to have anything more than his neighbor has, only deviations from the norm need be noted. General decisions require only a few indexes. Decisions in individual cases, however, demand that private details be probed in depth. If everyone should have the same, then investigating the individual is superfluous. If, on the other hand, the principle of to each his own is to be observed, then individual needs have to be examined. Justice leads inevitably to the erosion of the private.

Investigating data is one of the bureaucrat's normal duties. The most important aid has long been the information form or questionnaire, a sheet of paper with lines, fields, and boxes, on which everyone is supposed to enter his data. Although invented with the intention of allowing rapid and precise treatment of individual cases, information forms are primarily an instrument of bureaucratic information collection. Not only identity, marital status, and age are entered but also all sources of income, wealth, the property held by close relatives, home furnishings, and the contents of clothes closets. An individual can prove his need for welfare only by revealing his private living conditions. He can be offered a job only after he has listed his work record, his personal areas of knowledge, and his wishes. And a building permit can be granted only after both the plans and the builder have been approved . The authorities make their decisions based on forms that have been fully completed. The standardization of information accelerates work. Putting everything in writing ensures that decisions can be verified, and makes it possible to archive authorities' knowledge and preserve it for a long time.

Together, offices hold immense knowledge. Tax offices look into the turnover, property, expenditures, and revenues of firms and economic agents. Welfare offices record claims and benefits, health and employment data. School authorities keep files on achievements and tests, registration offices record residences and domiciles, the judicial authorities document offenses and crimes. By networking all this information one can arrive at an almost complete picture of the subject.

The development of the welfare state was accompanied by an explosion of data collection. To the extent that it cared for the poor, the elderly, and the sick, and ensured that everyone received the minimum required to survive, society was covered by a system of collection and distribution that subjected more and more areas of life to state information power. Concern about material subsistence and political stability eroded the private conduct of life. So long as public finances were still in the black, things did not depend on every detail. Generosity can get along with summary data. But the scarcer the resources, the stricter the control. Abuse can no longer be tolerated in any case. Financial need ineluctably entails further elaboration of the information apparatus.

A parallel development can be seen in the administration of the security state. Real and alleged dangers, terrorism, organized crime, uncontrolled immigration, political extremism, and religious fanaticism have put state organs on alert and caused a rapid expansion of surveillance. Unlike welfare authorities, security agents usually operate covertly. Wrongdoers are not supposed to have any idea that they are being tracked down. The ordinary citizen is subjected to eavesdropping and observation without his knowledge and against his will. Spies and investigators act like voyeurs with badges. Their curiosity is insatiable, because the state's suspicion of its citizens can never be fully dispelled. Anyone could be plotting a crime, anyone could deny the authorities the required obedience. For the security apparatus, an open society is ultimately a collection of shady figures, every brain is a fount of evil ideas, every private space a dark abyss whose furthest corners must be illuminated. The subject is always suspect. Hence the task of the security services is never done. They are constantly trying to improve spying. New groups are always coming into view, legal authority is continually being expanded, and if permission to proceed is ever denied, the services operate outside the rules when they deem it necessary. Data are to be stored for longer and longer periods so that no one can disappear without a trace into the thicket of society. Leviathan has enormous ears and eyes—and a long memory.

The evaluation of data is making rapid progress. Information power expands abruptly when scattered data can be personally attributed to an individual. Anonymous data about birth rates, leisure behavior, traffic volumes, or employment seem harmless enough. But as soon as individual aspects are combined in such a way as to point directly or indirectly to a person, the step toward the fully transparent subject has been taken. By networking various data banks it is not difficult to determine an individual's preferences, peculiarities, and habits, what paths he follows through the public sphere, whom he meets, with whom he speaks, and to what addresses he sends e-mail.

Networking data is in no way intended to probe into an individual's life. Ultimately the state is interested in understanding social networks. It wants to know what connections there are among its subjects, which groups, communities, sects, and cells exist. In addition to monitoring the individual, the state also monitors the social, the volatile intermediate realm of society that binds people together.

The government's ideal image of the completely transparent citizen is shared by the central institutions of economic society—with capitalistic business and commodity markets. Unlike the government, which is able to combine all its data to form a complete picture of the individual, the market's primary goal is not centralized registration. Every competitor would like to gain an advantage in information and keep data concerning his customers to himself. Not the all-powerful "Big Brother" but rather many little brothers are busy finding out people's secret wishes and activities.

In businesses, the first concern is to eliminate the unreliability of the labor force. Experts monitor the use of time, the work process, and the quality of the results. Although in a market economy firms are assigned to the private sector, personal motives, ideas, and wishes are dreaded disruptive factors. Since the early days of manufacturing, business discipline has meant subjecting the individual to an economy of time, continuity of work, and a supervisory hierarchy. Although modern management tries to make use of employees' personal needs, supervision of work still serves to put an end to individual tendencies. Private conversations must be conducted during breaks, not during work time; private thoughts distract from the work at hand; private concerns, feelings, and moods affect performance and the pace of work.

A whole arsenal of monitoring techniques may be used against underground private activities. Every telephone call can be recorded. Video cameras film personal contacts in the workplace. Small positioning devices communicate the identity of their bearers by means of biometric data and make it possible to monitor all movements within a building. At all times it is known where someone is—in the conference room, in the archive, with colleagues, in the canteen, in the bathroom. Computers allow work to be supervised more intensively without employees having to feel that a superior is constantly looking over their shoulders. Programs spy on computers and data, take regular screenshots, secretly record every keystroke, count errors, and register inactivity, the time during which the user enters nothing new on his computer.

On the commodity market other interests are dominant. Traders, banks, insurance companies, and advertising agencies collect information about customers in order to produce personal consumer profiles and open up new market niches. Anyone who knows his customers' buying habits can surprise them with special offers and try to bind them to him. The craving for information is considerable, for nothing seems more incalculable than shifts in the market, rises and declines in demand, the evolution of fashions, or changes in taste. A supplier who misses the boat in competing for customer data will fall behind. In order to open up new markets, precise data concerning target groups with special characteristics must be collected. If all the data regarding consumption that can be derived from a person's various credit cards, store cards, and automatic teller cards are combined, his birthdates, favorite newspaper, marital status, preferred brand of soap, and insurance discount can be determined. Without particularly bothering the customer, every one of his purchases is recorded in commercial databanks. Frequently consumers all too willingly agree to reveal their inclinations themselves. They fill out guarantee cards, use convenient service and bank cards, and in this way leave a broad trail behind them from which their wishes and habits, their travel routes, their telephone and mail contacts can be inferred.

Although it is praised as a realm of freedom, the market provides the individual with no protection against sellers' curiosity. To survive in a competitive environment, businesses have to constantly expand their databases. They need personal information in order to place each product and service upon whose sale their existence depends. Like the state, the market is no sanctuary of privacy. Its coercion just works indirectly. Commercial agencies are no less fertile in ideas than are government offices. Thus, in the end, the authorities rarely need to gather a great deal of data themselves. They can fall back on what private institutions have already collected. And sometimes companies offer these services themselves when a lucrative search assignment is in the offing. The unholy alliance of institutions ensures that the individual can no longer feel free from observation anywhere.

10 FREEDOM OF THOUGHT

Every power that wants to forego the use of the whip has to observe actions and guide thinking; it must keep an eye on what people do to eliminate dangerous connections and halt subversive acts. Surveillance supposedly tracks down suspicious clues and secrets in advance, but it reaches its limit at the surface of the human body. Observation can register written documents, conversations, and behavior, but it cannot read thoughts. People can always withdraw into their inner worlds, into the private realm of the imagination, to which no one else has direct access. Thought control is directed against this bastion. It does not seek to find out what people think but rather to impress on them what they can think. Observation generally comes too late. No video camera is able to prevent an offense. It can at most document what has already happened, and make it easier to prosecute. The politics of the mind, on the other hand, seeks to direct the future. It wants to uncover evil plans and guide thoughts in such a way that action follows the desired path.

Just as spying sometimes uses forceful means to extort information from bodies, so thought control operates in ways that are not always subtle or covert. Physical devices have always been used to implant ideas, feelings, and memories in the brain. The history of pedagogy, propaganda, and censorship is full of brutal repression, methods of punishment, suppression, humiliation, and accusation. The arsenal includes not only tempting rewards and inconspicuous manipulations. Today, the intellectual private sphere is still besieged by indoctrination. The goal is always the same: to shape ideas and perceptions, to control memory, feeling, and will. Thought control wants to penetrate beneath people's skin and lock them in an inner prison.

∽

The forms taken by the inner lack of freedom are manifold. In the prison of the senses, human beings are so flooded with stimuli that they can no longer process them all. Signals arouse attention, wishes flare up and then fade away. Spontaneous affect, not imagination or judgment, is in control. Driven by all sorts of temptations, humans are immersed in the whirl of events. They are in a peculiar way will-less, because impulses disappear as suddenly as the stimuli that elicited them. The driven person is what he is currently experiencing. He lacks the feeling that he has to decide about anything. And he lacks the certainty that he himself is the one who makes decisions and is responsible for them. He stumbles from one situation to another. The world takes him prisoner. The private inner space is completely occupied by external stimuli.

A brief flood of stimuli may be welcome. Allowing oneself to be driven through a sea of blinking lights, images, shop windows, and faces and, in so doing, forget oneself is a harmless pleasure so long as one has freely sought out this situation and can leave it again. However, enduring or jolting overstimulation that riddles perceptual defenses with holes leads to deformation. Large cities are not only the birthplace of modern privacy but also the site of mass consumption, arcades and shopping centers, glittering signs, constant waves of sound. Never before in the history of *Homo sapiens*, not even in the splendid palaces of despots, has there been a material environment in which people are confronted with so many acoustic stimuli at once. Generations of rural people from the provinces who came to the city for the first time felt overwhelmed by an environment that assailed them with sensual pleasures, broke through their defenses against stimuli, and at the same time aroused their greed. The perceptual powers of experienced city dwellers quickly adapted to this world. But even for them, the urban milieu has retained its ambivalent meaning. They can "immerse themselves" in the world and enjoy being caught up in the hustle and bustle. But sometimes they can also lose their bearings in the overfilled, deafening world and wander around with their heads buzzing.

The strategy of sensory deprivation opts for the opposite path. Before it became a preferred weapon of modern torture, many total institutions made use of a systematic poverty of stimuli. Individual cells and solitary confinement, a prohibition on speaking, sequestration, and isolation—these measures emptied out the environment and made people's minds submissive by ascetic means. Hunger was supposed to weaken the body, slow metabolism, make people think more slowly, and destroy imagination. The pain of emptiness was supposed to break the will and drive out wicked desires. A patient wearing down of the body purifies the mind, numbs the senses, and causes all thoughts directed toward the low temptations of the world to fade away. The prohibition on distractions and wild associations is strict. The outside world loses meaning. It is as if the world disappeared like soap bubbles. The senses are silenced, the mind falls into a deep loneliness, into a barren waste where words, images, and sounds no longer signify anything. Where there had been will and obstinacy, there is nothing left. Restlessness is gone, impulses are extinguished. Now the tabula rasa of the empty brain can be written upon anew.

Stimuli produce an effect only if people are receptive to them. Temptations presuppose that the victim will allow himself to be seduced. People can also voluntarily accept certain reductions in stimuli in order to arrive at another state of mind. Things are quite different in the dungeon of loyalty. The subject is governed by a will that works itself out behind his back. His imagination is not diluted as it is when the senses are oppressed. It is extremely active. The obedient subject constantly imagines what would happen if he did not do what is expected of him. He is threatened not by rashness and disorientation, emptiness and boredom, but rather by anxiety and a troubled conscience. He wants only what the other wants, and not because he himself wants it, but because the other wants it. The feeling of being bound by duty works like an invisible tyrant. Having a will of one's own seems a heinous infidelity, a social betrayal.

The subject is not the only one who serves a master. The life partner who has for years so neglected his own feelings and desires that he no longer even notices them also lives in the cage of loyalty. In symbiotic relationships the individual often has an astonishing ability to empathize with the person on whom he depends. He divines inner feelings before the other has even noticed them. He sees the world through the other's eyes and forgets to sharpen his own way of seeing it. He discerns the other's every wish but is incapable of still recognizing his own. He thinks what the other thinks, and over time has lost the ability to form thoughts of his own. Thus a sealed-off partnership hardens into an intimate world where the other is everything and the individual has disappeared into the common privacy.

Subjection obliterates independent thoughts. In contrast, indoctrination persuades people to act in accord with an alien will. Hackneyed ideas, phrases, formulas, and slogans clog the mind. Strong feelings are attached to fixed chains of associations. A word signal suffices to trigger a stereotyped series of formulas. The nation, the party, the leader, progress, solidarity, justice, the archenemy or rival—concrete affects and stereotypes are connected with all these imagined abstractions. The guiding figure is always farseeing, magnificent, resolute, and generous, even if he belongs to another world. The enemy is always dirty, disgusting, threatening, insidious, and cruel. The lackey of alien thought has no imagination and cannot envision any alternatives.

Not only do well-known institutions, sects and churches, parties and movements, preachers and agitators act as agents of indoctrination; apparently harmless institutions also engage in subtle brainwashing: school and family, the media, one's circle of friends, associations of like-minded people, the regulars at one's favorite bar. They share the same worldview, use the same clichés, think the same thoughts. Often it is a stifling world of ideas that have grown dull through endless repetition. Its supporters mouth the same empty phrases and become angry when an unusual expression comes up in the milieu where they live. Doctrinaire pedants insist that all methods and sources are identified in detail, meticulously check every reference and every footnote, and are confused if a new thought suddenly appears.

The conformist lives in a prison of fixed ideas. He does not realize that his ability to think has long since deteriorated. In contrast, the addict lives in the dungeon of the repetition compulsion. His thoughts are clear, his ability to take a distance on himself is intact, and yet he is driven by an alien force, an inner urge that is deaf to all the arts of persuasion. Despite all his intentions, despite his decision to abstain, against the recalcitrant will the mind is powerless. Addiction drives him to ruin, not because his will is too weak but because he is incapable of learning from experience. The addict's problem is the impotence of his judgments, not the frailty of his will. He is at the mercy of his addiction, and therefore he experiences his will not as a part of himself but rather as an independent, alien power. He can make all the resolutions he wants, and yet his addiction drives him back to work, to the gambling table, into intoxication. The imaginable possibilities are virtually boundless. Everything can become a drug, whether it is money, sex, adventure, or the thrill of being frightened. Under the spell of addiction people live a monotonous life. They are drawn into it again and again.

It cheats them of their future and kills their present. Experience makes them no wiser. The best intentions capitulate before the inner compulsion. Even after a successful withdrawal, a tiny temptation suffices, and the addict is once again what he was before. The addict is incapable of controlling himself. Warnings have no more effect than energetic resolutions. The will is stronger and locks the person within the inner cage.

External compulsions operate in the opposite way. They deprive a person of all free will. He experiences his thought and action as obligations. He has to impose something on himself, has to follow instructions, has to give in to a threat if he doesn't want to risk serious consequences. Unlike the addict, whose will eludes any understanding, reluctant action is commonly based on a clear weighing up of advantages and disadvantages. A person subjected to extortion does what he has to do, even though he doesn't want to do it. He does it because the cost of rebellion seems higher than that of obeying.

∾

Shaping people's minds often involves coercion. No cultural techniques can be communicated by curiosity, didactic finesse, and social arts of persuasion alone. Acquiring language, logic, and knowledge demands carefully worked-out methods. The politics of images and language impresses models of seeing, thinking, and talking on people. They are supposed to understand one another and share an obligatory system of ideas. The politics of memory constantly repeats the desired histories and excludes undesired memories.

What procedures does the politics of the mind use?
How do people end up in an inner cage where they are
no longer free? The ways are many and various, and today they are considered natural, innocuous cultural techniques. First of all, events and facts are associated with
unambiguous words and sorted into categories. This order
of things represents the elementary structure of collective knowledge. Multiple and overlapping meanings are
eliminated. Then these elements are bundled into handy
lessons, programs, or modules, ordered in sequences, and
communicated step by step. Specific tasks are assigned to
each level; their succession produces a verifiable ladder
of development. What is needed in pedagogy and didac-
tics is not free association, imaginative montages, or the
metaphors, analogies, and metonymies of undisciplined
thought, but rather clear classification, step-by-step sequences, and channeled thinking. Dissecting and com-
bining the elements produces a standardized knowledge
that everyone can learn, a manageable universe whose
boundaries are also the boundaries of the mind.

The regulation of language is part of the standardization
of the world picture. Manuals of correct usage, authorita-
tive decrees regarding vocabulary, grammar, and spelling,
continual monitoring of modes of expression used in the
family, in kindergartens, schools, and universities, in edito-
rial offices and administrations—the agents of the politics
of language are constant busy evaluating style and vocabulary, and telling contemporaries how to speak correctly.
Unseemly, repulsive, discrediting, or politically unpopu-
lar modes of speech are designated and banned. Instead,
euphemisms spread, reinterpreting facts or playing them

down. People who are fired from their jobs are said to be "released," apprentices are called "trainees," cripples are called "handicapped," threats are called "peace offers," and conquests are called "wars of liberation." Government intrusions into private life now "protect the citizen," provide "social justice," or serve "the common good." A tax hike is not considered an arbitrary political act but rather a "necessity of national policy."

Exercise follows standardization. It regularly sets graded tasks for the mind. The fetters of habit shackle free ability. The exercises are performed over and over until the material, the movement, or the formula has been so impressed on the individual that he can repeat it in his sleep. It is not convincing but drilling that destroys the uncomprehending individual's resistance. The repetitions are only occasionally voluntary. The fear of being humiliated or punished, the hope of receiving rewards and acknowledgment help the unwilling to make the leap. The dread of losing one's standing makes performance a social necessity.

Exercise is accompanied by the continual correction of errors. The latter may result from small mistakes, a moment of carelessness, a bit of bad luck, or an inability that can be overcome through repetition. A pupil who cannot recite the poem, the creed, the vocabulary, or the multiplication tables will be kept at them until he can do so without error. Or he will have to listen to the text repeated over and over until it has been pounded into him once and for all. When a teacher dictates a text, the red pencil and criticism loom. Correction says what is right and punishes mistakes with endless exercises. It establishes the norm by assigning sanctions for making errors. Even though contemporary pedagogy emphasizes the priority of social abilities, it can hardly get along without censuring students and humiliating them. Self-willed, quiet, or shy pupils are subjected to pressure to communicate just as lazy ones were once forced to do drills. They must learn to speak out so as not to disappoint their teachers; they have to practice social participation even if it is unsuitable for them. They are talked at until they begin to talk themselves; they are advised, analyzed, and treated therapeutically until their wills are so transformed that they no longer notice that it is an alien will that makes them put on a friendly face.

In order to be praised, the candidate must pass several tests. His progress is documented and evaluated. Examinations combine verification of knowledge with a ceremonial of power. They provide information about the student that is evaluated by the teacher alone. They make the student's knowledge visible and verify that he has the correct ideas. They register his achievements, abilities, and willpower, and record the results. His degree of knowledge is preserved in his file and compared to that of other students. In this monitoring of knowledge, supervision and tacit thought control are combined.

The politics of memory is concerned with correct memories. It selects the events that are to be thought about and abandons the rest to oblivion. The meaning of the past changes as the present moves on. Although the facts cannot be altered, history is constantly being rewritten. Myths and legends surround the foundation of states, nations, and institutions. They are impressed on every generation so that descendants know where they came from, who they are, and whom they must emulate. Private relationships also regularly fall back on memories when the reservoir of commonalities threatens to dry up. Memories strengthen cohesiveness and even out differences. If the feeling of belonging together disappears, the memory of past togetherness still remains.

The recollection of one's own defeats, misdeeds, or crimes is particularly delicate. Admonitions and ceremonies, appeals to shame or guilt, accompany work on the collective past. Crimes, at first, are generally denied, minimized, or not mentioned, and eventually they are forgotten. Individuals or collectives seldom recognize that they are to blame for the things they have done. Sometimes it takes years before they are ready to acknowledge the facts. But even obligatory duties to remember or belated admissions of guilt are of little use in bringing the soul back into balance and overcoming old resentments.

Defeats often provoke defiance or myths about a stab in the back. Other people are held responsible for the disgrace: foreigners, unpopular neighbors, fifth columnists. If national decline is connected with a major crime, a massacre or genocide, the catastrophe is not spoken of for a time, until people can celebrate recollecting it as a triumph of their own morality. People cheerfully treat the defeat as a liberation and march alongside the victors. In these historical images, all the private memories of offenses committed by the other side, of the victims in one's own family, of being driven out of one's homeland, of the destruction of cities are not welcome. Anyone who criticizes this truncated memory and sets private recollection alongside the official view is immediately suspected

of compensating, making tendentious excuses, or quali-
fying the unqualifiable. Standardized memory will not
tolerate other truths alongside its own. But in the long
run memories cannot be erased by either morality or disregard. They come back in the form of resentment, as
symptoms or—at best—as an accepted part of a complete
historical memory.

The agencies of thought control cannot feel secure so
long as human imagination has not been extinguished
and people's brains are still not fully programmable. In
the midst of conformism unwelcome memories survive,
unauthorized ideas develop, and writings are circulated
clandestinely. Heresy and dissidence, resistance and subversion, islands of private free thinking—all this would be
impossible had the government taken total control of our
inner worlds and already eradicated all free thoughts.

∾

For the nation's intellectual well-being, freedom of speech
and thought is indispensable. It prevents the pride of
dogmatism and protects us against the temptations of
self-righteousness. The feeling of one's own infallibility
is commonly based on the repression of other opinions.
Without contradiction there remains only the endless re-
iteration of the same ideas. Without a dialogue between
conflicting ideas the mental world congeals into formulas
and stereotypes. The more often an idea is repeated, the
more plausible it seems. Many convictions are based not
on conceptual clarity, empirical proof, and logical consis-
tency but rather on mere habit. Mental routines impress
slogans on the brain and block further reflection until fi-

nally ideas solidify into an ideology, speech into empty clichés, and the mind into a machine.

Only conflict can filter the truth out of the diversity of opinions. To recognize a description as true and a precept as right, there must be complete freedom to disapprove of it. It is only through criticism that people can—sometimes—become wiser, and only through the pain of error is the path to truth revealed to them. It is well known that the good part of making a mistake is that the next time one can avoid it.

That ideas can be proven and norms grounded to some extent does not justify censuring false or pernicious ideas. The abuse of the understanding is no reason to prohibit its further use. It is also no sign of courage to summarily forbid opinions considered dangerous, misleading, or immoral. There is a great difference between considering an opinion correct because it has withstood all attacks and considering it correct because no one has been allowed to contradict it. Obstinacy and unteachability do not justify any kind of prohibition on speech. Denying historical facts and ignoring overwhelming evidence is not a crime, only a form of idiocy. It is a matter not for the courts but for psychiatrists. Stupidity and propaganda are countered not with censorship but with all the means of public controversy. A judgment becomes persuasive because it can be corrected if it turns out to be false. But this presupposes that the means of correction are already in place, and that everyone is free to speak and think as he wishes.

As the history of ideas shows, the truth only seldom triumphs over power and persecution. To think that the truth sooner or later comes out on its own is to indulge in

historical sentimentality. For centuries, stifling supersti-
tions and mental tyranny prevented generations of people
from making independent use of their reason. Prohibitions on thinking and fashionable prattle still lull many
people in wooly foolishness. Because people are just as
receptive to errors as to truths, they need freedom of
thought. Only contradiction can protect them against
credulity and mental sluggishness.

∽

Freedom of thought must not be curtailed in any way.
Even the most sacred things are not to be honored before
the Devil has had his say against them. But since the evil
advocate is always able to think of further objections, absolute certainty can never be achieved. He is also allowed
to go to extremes, to make use of polemics, mockery, or
slander. A sentimental plea for tolerance and decorum is
merely an attempt to protect one's own cowardice.

The most important arena of intellectual controversy
used to be religion. In order to put an end to civil war, belief was declared to be a private matter, and for a time this
took the edge off religious antagonisms. Since freedom
of belief has been guaranteed, many people consider the
question settled. Instead of criticism and polemics, the
spirit of the time demands dialogue, understanding, for-
bearance, and good behavior. Given the drama of religious
experiences, the mob of semi-believers, rites, and myths,
the questionable evidence of divine revelation can hardly
be dealt with seriously by anyone. Many people find an
overt statement of religious belief simply embarrassing.
Uneasiness about the disenchanted modern world is not

fertile soil for the growth of a new religious faith. The upwelling of religiosity during the changing of the guard in the Vatican had less to do with religion than with the masses' changing feelings about authoritarian pageantry. In any case, enlightened contemporaries no longer want to waste time on the fund of traditional theological subtleties. Obscure pieties, liturgical pomp, or fanatical enthusiasm elicit at best a baffled shake of the head. But that does not suffice to overcome the need for spirituality or to ward off attacks on privacy and freedom of thought.

Criticism of religion is in no way finished. The explosive nature of current conflicts is no reason to shelter from human judgment the religious myths, doctrines, and forms of worship that people have created and handed down. The insight that demons and gods are created by humans would be untrue were it not applied as well to the one all-powerful God. It is well known that images of God are ideas about things that people can believe in but that they ultimately can know nothing about. Blasphemy is thus logically impossible, even if people who claim to believe fervently in their respective gods feel personally offended. Regarding something whose existence is, in principle, indeterminable one can say anything and nothing at all. In no case can a single true or false description of a reality that exists independently of the belief of those who practice these discourses be deduced from metaphorical discourse about God.

Hardly more credible is the idea that the highest divinity is at the same time all-powerful, just, and merciful. How can the tiresome problem of evil be resolved? Either the omnipotent God wants to eliminate vice and evil and he can't, or he can and doesn't want to, or he doesn't want to and can't, or he will and can. If he wants to and can't, then he is weak, powerless, the opposite of a god. If he can and doesn't want to, then he is malevolent, vengeful, malicious, which God in general should not be. If he doesn't want to and can't, then he is both malevolent and weak, and therefore not God. But if he wants to and can, why is there evil in the world and why doesn't he eliminate it? There is still more: if God is merciful and just, why is an infinite punishment imposed for a finite human guilt so that a human sacrifice is needed to redeem everyone? Such a disproportionate means is extremely ill suited to reconciliation and justice.

Fervent adoration of a sacred idol can never be overcome by such logical considerations. Still less is it likely to be influenced by malicious gossip or mocking, blasphemous verses and caricatures. Popular talk about the "injury done to religious feelings" disregards the essence of religious experience. That people believe they have to rush to the aid of their God has nothing to do with true piety. On the contrary: it is an unparalleled presumption. Gods and prophets cannot possibly be sullied by pictures. Only someone who has demoted his gods to men could imagine that he has to defend them against other people's attacks. The true believer stands far above such profane activities. Holy wrath seizes true believers less than it does semi-believers who feel mocked because they are no longer convinced of their own convictions. Bigotry, fanaticism, and violence have their grounds not in religious fervor but in the fragility of a faith that doesn't really want to believe. Someone truly secure in his religious belief doesn't need to howl in pain, roar for vengeance, burn people at the stake, or wear a suicide belt.

Dogmas, mottos, ceremonies, and taboos are no more than a religion's mausoleum. A faith worthy of the name is not a kind of sermonizing humanism. Religion is a taste for the infinite, the invisible, and the super-powerful. It is not rooted in literal interpretation, in zealous obedience, facile consolation, or pressure to do good deeds. Religious faith is based on the experience of the holy. The visible world appears to be a part of a higher, spiritual universe from which it derives its meaning. The believer is moved by the divine, whether in an event of personal revelation, in moments of selfless ecstasy, rapture, silent prayer, or meditation, or through collective rites in which the original religious experience is renewed. Religion is not an option but rather an inner compulsion. One cannot join a faith the way one can join a church or a party. The true believer has no choice. The experience of the holy is not based on his free decision. For him, the revelation of the divine is immediately self-evident.

Even if belief in God is intellectually difficult to maintain, the need for spirituality is widespread. People repeatedly find that what happens to them and what results from their acts does not depend on themselves alone. Some people therefore believe that supernatural powers are responsible for their fate, for their birth, existence, and death. Cases of rescue, healing, good fortune, and disaster seem to point to a power that one can thank, implore, or curse. Only this power can free one from the burden of mortality, give profane life an inner goal and suffering a higher meaning. The need for security and meaning, for overcoming the self, and for the illusion of immortality has always been the breeding ground for the religious bond. But the desire to believe in something is not a sufficient reason for belief, only for wishful thinking. Worse yet, an opinion based solely on a wish inevitably leads to denial of the facts. The only reason that belief in a higher being is not simply a form of hallucination is that its object lies in the supersensory realm and is immune to empirical evidence. One can believe in gods with impunity, and without losing oneself in a world of madness.

The desire for meaning and immortality is also the gateway to a mission. Dialogue between religions is not aimed at a friendly exchange of ideas leading to mutual harmony. The idea that dialogue and respect between denominations and religions is always possible because all people allegedly feel the same spiritual need is nothing but a myth. In the conflict between religions, tolerance or peace is not at issue but rather the primacy of one's own revelation. The religious word is the Word of God. It does not proclaim to those with different beliefs something entirely unknown to them but instead makes clear to them the hidden meaning of something of which they had long been vaguely aware. Only someone who has completely lost touch with the experience of the holy and considers a life pleasing to God a purely private matter can seriously expect from religious discourse a tranquil recognition of all departures from the true path.

Religion intensifies certainty in areas where one can neither see nor prove. It produces firm convictions when something is not inherently plausible. Hence the tendency to dogmatism. It protects doctrines whose contradiction would lead to abyssal uncertainty. The power of doubt calls for pure doctrine. Anyone to whom the self-evidence of the holy is denied persists all the more pig-headedly in secondhand piety. He defends tooth and nail the witness, the authority of the representative or prophet. Such semi-belief constantly appears along with an aggressive demand for compliance. Since it lacks the ultimate security provided by the gift of grace, it needs the support of hope and literality. It will never accept a sphere of private convictions. Semi-belief accepts no compromises, and it is notoriously easy to offend. The religious zealot can take words and images only literally. Double meanings such as those involved in jokes, satire, or irony destabilize his image of the divine. Semi-believers find little to laugh at.

The anger of supporters and semi-believers cannot be taken as a touchstone for determining what can be expressed in a society. Every attack that is found difficult to parry ignites passions, triggers outbreaks of rage, and feeds resentments. But that is no reason to limit freedom of speech and thought to an allegedly fair degree. Where are the limits to be set? The losers' rancor provides no guideline for self-censorship. Rudeness, sarcasm, distortions, and slanders are part of controversy about opinions, just as are malice, zealotry, and impatience. They can be fought only insofar as people are free to speak out against them, to contradict tactless remarks. A freedom that cannot be abused is not a freedom. Freedom does not include the duty always to think correctly and always to do what is good. Malicious words and deeds are not a result of freedom, they are proof of it.

Some supporters of fashionable cultural relativism are nonetheless prepared to forego freedom and truth. In the name of harmony and concord, of peace, and even of privacy, they would like to leave people with different beliefs alone, whether out of fear, indifference, or superficiality. They confuse religion and ideology with private matters, although every ideology strives to raze the fortress of privacy and turn everyone into an obedient and happy supporter. Intellectual cowardice paves the way for those who have put any free ideas on their Index.

Freedom of belief and thought guarantees freedom for every faith, for revelations and religious ways of life of every variety. But it also guarantees freedom from every implausible belief, from every religion and illusion. It never entails the duty to forego knowledge and truth for the sake of a belief. No religion is sacrosanct. An individual can believe whatever he wants, but he cannot expect others to consider sacred what he considers sacred. He can try to persuade others to adopt his beliefs, but he cannot count on his beliefs being exempt from criticism and having a claim to special protection. The right to privacy puts an end to the imperialism of religion. No one has an obligation to live in accord with the will of a God or with any particular religious request, or even to respect them.

∾

Freedom of mind provides protection against hasty agreement, false harmony, and the slumber of uncontested opinion. A consensus that thinks it can get along without proofs ends in conformism, dependency, and obedience. The grounds for an assertion consist in large part in a refutation of the apparent grounds for the opposing opinion. One can only really possess a truth when one can defend it actively and promptly recognize the enemies of freedom.

Laziness, cowardice, and indifference are still the most important causes of dependency. It is not social conditions, worn-out educational systems, or the secular depreciation of old values that are responsible for the fact that people continue to doze in conformism. They are themselves to blame for their dependency. Many people feel more comfortable being dependent. They are too lazy to use their understanding and prefer to let others make decisions. They allow others to speak, think, and act for them, and withdraw into the cage of passivity. On the other hand, cowards immediately take to their heels when conflict breaks out. If they sense contradiction, they complain about a lack of tolerance. Moral cowards always prefer people who share their ideas and are on their same level. They would rather throw themselves to the floor than stand up to attacks. Indifferent types ultimately make themselves blind and deaf. If a misdeed or misfortune occurs near them, they shrug their shoulders and go on their way. They want to remain in their corners, just as they are. Alarms warn them of impending danger so that they can avert their eyes in time. They prefer to become indignant, because indignation costs them nothing and complaining about others justifies their own inactivity. No change in customs or social reform will do away with these vices and bad habits; they can be eliminated only when individuals undergo a personal revolution. Anyone who, of his own accord, lays down the weapons of criticism also allows his power of judgment and decision to decay. In the end, he should not be surprised by his existence as a fully transparent subject. His private sphere has long since disappeared. He always leaves behind the same traces. He no longer needs to be observed and investigated, since everyone knows what he is thinking and doing anyway.

Notes

1 TRACES

An inevitable consequence of extensive surveillance is the
rapid growth of databanks and archives. A society subjected to
complete surveillance would never sleep. It would never forget anything. A society that knows too much becomes obsessed
with surveillance but cannot act. Therefore, one of the most
beneficial discoveries of the computer culture is the delete key.
It facilitates the work of those concerned with cancellations.
Documents no longer need to be torn up, shredded, or burned.
A single keystroke can suffice to destroy data. This frees society
from excessive supervision. (Cf. H. Loetscher, "Ein Rückblick
auf unser Jahrhundert von einem pazifischen Ufer aus," in *Die
Weltwoche*, 17 November 1983, where he expresses the subversive idea of an "international deletion festival" involving delete
keys being pressed worldwide on New Year's Eve 1999, with bil-
lions of shocked computers responding, "Are you sure you want
to delete this file?" The answer was yes.)

A telescreen must not be confused with a television. In
George Orwell's *1984* a telescreen served as a sending and receiving device. It was a microphone, video camera, alarm clock,
radio, movie screen, and television set rolled into one. That was
already a technical advance over the loudspeakers and the pink,
swinging membranes that, earlier, had registered the conversations of people walking down the streets and transmitted them

to the security office (cf. J. Samjatijn, *Wir* [Zürich, 1977]). In Samjatijn's transparent city, these listening devices had the same function as video cameras on city squares and at intersections. However, if literary parallels are sought, the present situation resembles less Bentham's, Orwell's, Huxley's, or Samjatijn's scenarios than it does the world of Kafka's novel *The Trial*. The offensive self-staging practiced by many contemporaries has led some media observers to attribute to surveillance a constitutive role in the development of personal identity. Cf., for example, M. Schroer, "Sehen und gesehen werden. Von der Angst vor Überwachung zur Lust an der Beobachtung?" in *Merkur* 57, no. 646 (2003). That a handful of young people make a game out of going on a rampage in front of surveillance cameras is explained by nothing other than the old, familiar pleasure of provocation. That many amateurs acting in front of television cameras do not even notice how ridiculous they appear indicates more a complete absence of shame and judgment than problems with identity. Cat-and-mouse games, public indiscretions, ambition, the need for recognition, and provocative tests of courage are not new. Even the fear of being overlooked is not exactly novel. No doubt the stages the media provides favor disregard for social distance. But society in general cannot be reduced to a media society or an information society. Data, knowledge, and communication are only one aspect of the social. Anyone who places them in the center of his diagnosis of our time ignores not only the harder, physical aspects of society but also overlooks the other dimensions of the private and fails to appreciate the importance of the structures that make expanded surveillance a genuine political danger.

2 POWER AND PRIVACY

Domination differs from other forms of power in that the subject complies with the master's will. The fixation on the problem of legitimacy has led people to overlook the variety and banality of other motives for obeying. In the long run, a ruler finds that he is obeyed only because his subjects consider his superiority justified. Sometimes it is pure fear or dull habit that keeps people in long-term slavery. Domination must also not have already crystallized into institutions. If a religious, military, or political leader finds a true following, this is already a form of domination. His instructions and commands are promptly obeyed. Overt surveillance carried out by the secret police is a proven method of nonviolent terror. For example, the "state security" forces in the former German Democratic Republic did not limit themselves to the ostentatious presence of their investigators. Observers also used video cameras to record their victim's every movement. Thus it sometimes happened that the subject under surveillance, the "target," looked directly into the camera, knowing full well that he was being observed and photographed. Consequently, anyone who let it be known that he had noticed the photographer only increased the suspicion. And anyone who tried to evade the camera's view convicted himself. On this, see K. Hartewig, *Das Auge der Partei. Fotografie und Staats-sicherheit* (Berlin 2004). Economic advantages play a not insignificant role in the stability of dictatorships. The majority of the population usually benefits from the expropriation of persecuted minorities, plundering raids inside and outside the country's borders, or from the generous distribution of public goods, so long as it does not lead to new tax burdens. Machiavelli recommended long ago that the ruler should be moderately generous to the majority, from whom he could take nothing, and sparing with the few to whom he could give nothing (*The Prince*, chap. 16). On the shocking overreaction of democratic societies to external and internal subversion, see E. Schill's classic study written immediately after the McCarthy era: *The Torment of Secrecy: The Background and Consequences of American Security Policies* (Glencoe, Ill., 1956). If the sense for the private is not well established and energetic intervention has not become a political tradition, then officials

obviously tend to conspiratorial security measures instead of in-
forming the public of what they know and also of what they do
not know. On the cultural history of surveillance from the eye of
God to satellite cameras, see the rich catalog drawn up by Th. Y.
Levin et al., eds., *CTRL-space: Rhetorics of Surveillance from
Bentham to Big Brother* (Cambridge, Mass., 2002).

3   RETROSPECTIVES

On the history of the private, Philippe Ariès and Georges Duby's
The History of Private Life, 5 vols. (Cambridge, Mass.: Harvard
University Press, 1987–91), remains unsurpassed. This general
study, which I have frequently consulted, confirms the insight
that historical change can be meaningfully narrated only if one
presupposes the existence of social and anthropological uni-
versals. The beginnings of bourgeois privacy are portrayed in
Christoph Heyl's remarkable study, *A Passion for Privacy. Untersuchungen zur Genese der bürgerlichen Privatsphäre in London
(1660–1800)* (Munich, 2004). Countless empirical indications
of the cultural universality of the private sphere are provided
by H. P. Duerr's massive work, *Der Mythos vom Zivilisation-
sprozeß*, 5 vols. (Frankfurt, 1988–2002); on imaginary walls,
see "Nacktheit und Scham," §10 (Frankfurt, 1988); on the
function of shame about the body, see, in particular, "Intim-
ität," §16 (Frankfurt, 1990). The origin of the idea of discipline
in the West is obviously not Jeremy Bentham's "Panopticon"
but rather the Roman military tradition and Rule of St. Bene-
dict, the Abbot of Monte Cassino. Cf. H. U. von Balthasar, *Die
großen Ordensregeln* (Einsiedeln, 1961), 175–259. Later devel-
opments in organizational discipline are discussed by, among
others, Karl Marx, *Das Kapital*, 1:13, 4; Michel Foucault, *Discipline and Punish: The Birth of the Prison* (New York, 1977); and
Erving Goffmann, *Asylums: Essays on the Social Situation of
Mental Patients and Other Inmates* (Garden City, N.Y., 1961).

4 FREEDOM AND PRIVACY

On the concept of negative freedom, see Isaiah Berlin, *Four Essays on Liberty* (New York and London, 1969). For any debate on the functions of the state, the classic work by Wilhelm von Humboldt, *The Limits of State Action* (1792; London, 1969), is indispensable. Humboldt formulates all the objections to the inner imperialism of modern state power. In *The Value of Privacy* (Malden, Mass., 2005), Beate Rössler assesses privacy at a very high level, grounding it in autonomy, authenticity, self-determination, and self-reflection. But these are postulates that forego the modest achievements of negative freedom. Privacy is first of all "freedom from," not "freedom to (do something)." Rössler's instructive argument begins from the intuition that private freedoms require, given welfare state and communitarian demands, a special normative foundation, and that this is valid only if it can be derived from higher ends. However, if freedom is understood as merely a means to an end and not an end in itself, then it can be justified only if it serves some supposedly higher end. As if, ultimately, the only person who deserves a bit of freedom is the one who explicitly asks who he is and how he wants to live. On the contrary, it must be recognized that the absence of coercion and external meddling is primary for private freedom. Whether a subject makes use of the options that will in any case arise by themselves in situations where there is no coercion, whether he develops abilities or even wants to reflect on his possibilities at all, is of secondary importance for the value of privacy. What is crucial is that no one prescribes what he must do and think. Anonymity has an effect on the ways of proving nobility. Whereas courtly etiquette demanded detailed compliments for specific individuals, in the cities a repertory of formalistic phrases developed that were applicable to everyone. Thus being nameless amid strangers did not mean a heartless alienation but rather a standardization of courtesy for many situations. Cf. Richard Sennett, *The Fall of Public Man* (New York, 1976), chap. 3. On

136 NOTES

etiquette at the court of Versailles, see also Norbert Elias, *The Court Society* (New York, 1983), chap. 5.

5 TERRITORIES OF THE SELF

The primal scene of the fear of being touched is the anthropological starting point for Elias Canetti's *Crowds and Power* (London 1962). On the territories of the self and their violation, see, especially, Erving Goffman, *Relations in Public: Microstudies of the Public Order* (New York, 1971). On the phenomenology of disgust, see Aurel Kolnai, *On Disgust* (Chicago, 2004). On the proper evaluation of courtliness and the civilizing value of appearance, see Immanuel Kant, *Anthropology from a Pragmatic Point of View* (1798; New York, 2006); Jean de La Bruyère, *Characters* (1688; London 1963), especially the chapter titled "On Society and Conversation"; Arthur Schopenhauer, *The Wisdom of Life* (1886; London 1917); Henri Bergson, "La politesse," in *Ecrits et paroles*, Vol. 1 (Paris, 1957); (André) Alain, *Alain on Happiness* (New York, 1973).

6 SECRETS OF THE BODY

A comprehensive cultural and art history of the feeling of shame is offered not only by H. P. Duerr but also by Jean-Claude Bologne, *Histoire de la pudeur* (Paris, 1986). On the theory of shame, cf. H. Landweer, *Scham und Macht: Phänomenologische Untersuchungen zur Sozialität eines Gefühls* (Tübingen, 1999). Shame is a self-relationship like the somatic or cognitive self-relationship. All these forms of self-relationship can be broadened into a social behavior, but their structure is not itself social or communicative. Someone who talks to himself is not telling himself anything, nor does he arrive at an understanding with himself as two individuals might. Someone who feels pain does not assume the place of another person in order to observe that his tooth or his stomach hurts. Someone who blushes with shame does not see himself with others' eyes but with his own. And only because he does so can he also see himself from another's viewpoint. In a culture characterized by intrusive publicity, the awareness that secrecy is a fundamental form of the social seems to be waning. Cf. Georg Simmel, *Soziologie. Untersuchungen über die Formen der Vergesellschaftung*, chap. 5 (Frankfurt, 1992). Alain Corbin offers many diverse observations in his essay, "Backstage," in Michele Perrot, ed., *The History of Private Life*, Vol. 4, *From the Fires of Revolution to the Great War* (Cambridge, Mass., 1990); cf. also Gérard Vincent, "A History of Secrets?" in Antoine Prost and Gérard Vincent, eds., *The History of Private Life*, Vol. 5, *Riddles of Identity in Modern Times* (Cambridge, Mass., 1991). In addition to the psychiatric and sociological literature on suicide, see J. Améry, *Hand an sich legen. Diskurs über den Freitod* (Stuttgart, 1976), and the study by M. Pinguet, *La mort volontaire au Japon* (Paris, 1984), which received far too little notice. Ch. Geyer has edited an overview of the debate on biopolitics, titled *Biopolitik. Die Positionen* (Frankfurt, 2001).

7   PRIVATE SPACES

On the history of hygiene, the dwelling, and the cleansing of cities, see U. Dirlmeier et al., eds., *Geschichte des Wohnens*, 5 vols. (Stuttgart, 1996–1999); M. Frey, *Der reinliche Bürger. Entstehung und Verbreitung bürgerlicher Tugenden in Deutschland 1760–1860* (Göttingen, 1997); P. Payer, *Der Gestank von Wien. Über Kanalgase, Totendünste und andere üble Geruchskulissen* (Wien, 1997); and A. Corbin, *The Foul and the Fragrant: Odor and the French Social Imagination* (Cambridge, Mass., 1986). In his *The Condition of the Working Class in England* (New York, 1993), Friedrich Engels reported on the quarters where the early industrial proletariat lived. Martin

Heidegger uses the concept of *Zuhandenheit* ("readiness to hand") to characterize the unquestionable reliability of private everyday objects. They are inconspicuous, unintrusive, unrebellious, and therefore the body can move effortlessly among them; see *Being and Time* (New York, 1962), §§ 15, 16. On spatial transitions, see Arnold van Gennep, *Rites of Passage* (Chicago, 1960), chap. 3. On the introduction of video cameras in various social situations, see L. Hemel and J. Metelmann, *Bild- Raum–Kontrolle. Videoüberwachung als Zeichen gesellschaftlichen Wandels* (Frankfurt, 2005).

8   PROPERTY

On the critique of property since Aristophanes, see A. Künzli, *Mein und Dein. Zur Ideengeschichte der Eigentumsfeindschaft* (Cologne, 1986). The fable is found at the beginning of Jean-Jacques Rousseau's *Discourse on the Origin of Inequality* (1754). Which distribution of property is considered just is a fundamental political question, the answer to which depends not least upon which concept of justice and equality is adopted. Should every individual have the same as every other, as much as he needs, as he earns, or as he himself thinks would be justified? David Hume long ago indicated the disastrous social consequences of a formal, equal distribution of property in his *Enquiry Concerning the Principles of Morals* (1751). An interesting and at the same time elegant way of escaping from the discourse on equality, need, well-being, or social utility is offered by a theory that grounds the claim to property historically. According to this theory, people have a legitimate right to the property that they have acquired in legitimate ways—through trade, purchase, labor, or gifts. In this property relationship no state has the right to tax or redistribute unless these measures serve to create or maintain the conditions indispensable for free transactions. Any redistribution of legally acquired property is not only an impermissible encroachment upon the individual's freedom but is also a gross injustice. On this view, see Robert Nozick, *Anarchy, State, and Utopia* (New York, 1974). On the history of the modern fiscal state, cf. the colorful description in W. Reinhard, *Geschichte der Staatsgewalt. Eine vergleichende Verfassungsgeschichte Europas von den Anfängen bis zur Gegenwart* (Munich, 1999), chap. 4.

9 INFORMATION

Reginald Whitaker, in *The End of Privacy: How Total Surveillance Is Becoming a Reality* (New York, 1999), offers an overview of new techniques used by information power. Particularly instructive regarding the current situation is D. J. Solove's prudent analysis, *The Digital Person: Technology and Privacy in the Information Age* (New York, 2004), which avoids popular alarmism. The problem of how to protect data and social information arose long before the technologizing of data collection and the establishment of databanks. The protection of privacy and the distribution of personal knowledge are involved in every social contact. The methods of self-presentation and personal information politics are investigated in Erving Goffman's *The Presentation of Self in Everyday Life* (1956; rpt. New York, 1992); *Interaction Ritual: Essays on the Face-to-Face Behavior* (New York, 1967); and *Stigma: Notes on the Management of Spoiled Identity* (Englewood Cliffs, N.J., 1963). How one gives others a false idea of what is going on right in front of them and with whom they are dealing, is shown by Goffman's analysis of deception in *Frame Analysis: An Essay on the Organization of Experience* (Cambridge, Mass., 1974), chaps. 4–6. On the structure and methods of gossip, see Norbert Elias and J. L. Scotson, *The Established and the Outsiders: A Sociological Enquiry into Community Problems* (London, 1965), as well as J. R. Bergmann, *Klatsch. Zur Sozialform der diskreten Indiskretion* (Berlin, 1987). On classical data collection by means of forms, see Rainer Paris,

Normale Macht. Soziologische Essays (Konstanz, 2005). On the dynamics of the security state, see also W. Sofsky, *Das Prinzip Sicherheit* (Frankfurt, 2005).

10 FREEDOM OF THOUGHT

For the idea of a typology of inner "unfreedoms" and the corresponding social figures, I am indebted to P. Bieri, *Das Handwerk der Freiheit. Über die Entdeckung des eigenen Willens* (Frankfurt, 2003), chap. 4. The complaint about the flood of stimuli is undoubtedly one of the most popular topoi of conservative cultural criticism. Even if it does not allow us to grasp the core of the modern experience of civilization, that does not alter the fact that people occasionally experience this sort of thing. The literary history of the city includes countless descriptions of the perceptual shock that awaits visitors to a great metropolis. On freedom of thought, see the still useful guide in the second chapter of John Stuart Mill's *On Liberty* (1859). On the structure of "semi-belief," see R. Paris, *Normale Macht* (Konstanz, 2005). The irritation regarding the "return of religion" that some enlightened contemporaries have experienced is bothersome not least because venerable criticisms of religion have apparently fallen into oblivion. Only a few people seem prepared even to approach the phenomenon of religious experience. However, anyone who does not perceive the seriousness of religious belief is poorly equipped for the controversies currently raging. On the experience of the holy, see the classical texts by William James, *The Varieties of Religious Experience* (New York, 1902); Roger Caillois, *Man and the Sacred* (1959; rpt. Westport, Conn., 1980); Rudolf Otto, *The Idea of the Holy: An Inquiry into the Non-rational Factor in the Idea of the Divine and Its Relation to the Rational* (1917; New York, 1958); Friedrich Schleiermacher, *On Religion: Speeches to Its Cultured Despisers* (1799; New York, 1996).